Methadone

Methadone

J. Bennett Brown

TATE PUBLISHING
AND ENTERPRISES, LLC

Published by Tate Publishing & Enterprises, LLC
127 E. Trade Center Terrace | Mustang, Oklahoma 73064 USA
1.888.361.9473 | www.tatepublishing.com

Tate Publishing is committed to excellence in the publishing industry. The company reflects the philosophy established by the founders, based on Psalm 68:11,
"The Lord gave the word and great was the company of those who published it."

Book design copyright © 2014 by Tate Publishing, LLC. All rights reserved.
Cover design by Jim Villaflores
Interior design by Jake Muelle

Published in the United States of America
ISBN: 978-1-63367-246-8
Biography & Autobiography / Personal Memoirs
14.10.10

Katy, this book is dedicated to you, Katy Lou Nicholas (1945–1986). Katy, you were and always will be very special to me. Of all my siblings, you and I were connected in a very special way. You were like a second mother to all of us, your sisters and brothers. It is because of the promise that I made to you, *Methadone* was written. I kept the story as true as I told it to you twenty-eight years ago. Find a special tree in heaven, and read it along with the rest of the world.

To my wife, Phyllis, you are and always will be the woman of my dreams. Your love for me has made me a better man. My love for you is every breath I take. It is my life. When God gave you to me, he gave me the best he had to offer.

To my sister Selenia, if it were not for you and the man you married, Richard Johnson, I would have no story to share. I love you with all my heart.

And to all of those that went before me, I told the story of *Methadone*, rest in peace.

Contents

Prologue

First, I must tell you I am not a writer; I just had a story to tell about a time in my life when I made the wrong choice when I faced my fork in the road. That choice would have cost me my life if it were not for the grace of God. I wrote this book twice. The first time I wrote it, I read it and realized how much wisdom I put into the book. It read like me at sixty instead of at eighteen. At eighteen, I didn't have much wisdom. I never read the Bible numerous times. I never read Deepak Chopra, Watchman Nee, the life story of Smith Wigglesworth, and the many other books I have read now. So I wrote it over again from the mind of an eighteen-year-old.

I will not say this is a true story, so read the book and afterward draw your own conclusions. What I can say is, it would be awfully hard to imagine this story.

My sister Katy was diagnosed with breast cancer in 1986 and died a few months later.

I was living in Winston-Salem, North Carolina at the time of her illness. Her doctors had given her a few months to live, so I traveled to Detroit to spend some time with her. One day as she and I were talking, she asked me this question, "What happened in Washington, DC, that caused your personality to change so drastically? You went from a young boy with a playful personality to a young man with the wisdom of an old man, with an unshakeable faith in God. When you and I would sit and talk, there was a sparkle in your eyes, like you had a secret no one else knew about."

Each day, I visited the hospital. I sat by her bed and told her this story. She would remember the last word I spoke the day before and would remind me when I sometimes tried to skip forward to make the story short. "Don't leave anything out," she would say to me. "I need to know everything that happened!" It took five days for me to complete the story. I tried each day not to tire her out with my long visits, but when I stopped and said, "I will tell you more tomorrow," she would not want me to stop. Once I completed the story, she suggested I write a book about it. I told Katy that she was the only person I've ever shared this story with. And not talking about this story, I believe, is what is keeping me alive. "One day, the time will be right," she said, "Promise me you will write this book, and let history be the judge." I told her I would. Katy passed away three months after our time together. Twenty seven years later, I decided to keep my promise. Most of the people involved in this story have passed away. And unless they told a family member this story, they would never connect the dots. I would like to say, I did not write this book to glorify the choice I made when I faced my fork in the road; I hope, by telling my story, it may help anyone who is faced with a decision that could affect the rest of their life. I say, don't take the shortcut as I did because the choice may seem easy and appear to give you the same results when it never does.

It is the path to destruction...As a young boy growing up in Mississippi in the '50s, I decided one thing that is "I would never be poor." I remember working in cotton fields for three dollars a day from sunup to sundown. We were taught if you got a good education, there was a very good chance you would not be poor. Upon graduating from high school, I was given the choice, to live with my sister Katy in Detroit and attend Michigan State or move to Washington, DC, with my sister Selenia and attend

Howard University. After visiting my sister Katy in Detroit and my sister Selenia in Washington DC, I chose to attend Howard.

My mother raised seven children without a husband. She taught us the importance of great character. To tell a lie or do anything to offend God was unforgiveable. We attended the Church of God in Christ.

And our family was there whenever the door was open. That is why the choice I made in the summer of 1972 was so shameful and almost cost me my life for the sin I committed. But God had another plan.

The History of Methadone

Methadone is a narcotic painkiller, similar to morphine. It reduces the pain of withdrawal suffered by individuals addicted to heroin. It is a synthetic opioid with a long-acting medication effect that allows heroin addicts longer periods between injections while treating the effects of heroin addiction. It gives you the same high as heroin without craving the addiction. Ultimately, methadone treats and cures heroin addiction.

German World War II soldiers were given heroin injections by the government to numb the effects of war. Methadone was invented in Germany in 1937 to counter the effects of the addictions created by the use of heroin.

After World War II, the American soldiers returned home with heroin addictions. Over 90 percent were treated with methadone and returned to their communities as productive citizens. The methadone program was labeled as saving the dignity of the American war veteran after World War II.

During the Vietnam War, many American soldiers returned home with heroin addictions in greater numbers ever created in World War II, but unlike the World War II soldiers, they did not seek treatment at the many methadone treatments centers put in place across the country. In 1972, crime in every major city had increased as a result of heroin-addicted war veterans not responding to the methadone program. It reached to a point in 1972 where it was declared by the Nixon administration.a threat to national security. What they did next to address this problem is what this book is all about. Many lost their lives. Some were friends of mine.

The Move to Washington, DC

For many years, I have been reluctant to tell this story. I have only told it to one other person, my sister Katy, who is now deceased. She told me I should write a book and tell the story to the world and let history be the judge. So I decided to tell the story after many of the people involved had passed away.

It started in 1972, when I was eighteen and fresh out of high school. My sister Katy lived in Detroit, and my sister Selena lived in Washington, DC. They both wanted me to come and live with them. Both cities sounded exciting to me! You see, my family moved to New Orleans from Mississippi when I was fourteen, and the only question I asked my mother when she informed all of us that we were moving there was "Are there any cotton fields in New Orleans?" She told me no. I was ready to move to New Orleans! I hated cotton fields! When I was very little, around five or six, I cried when my sisters would leave me and go to the cotton fields. When I got old enough to go to the fields, I cried not to go. The cotton fields and church was all I remembered about Mississippi. When we were not at church, we were in the cotton fields. My grandmother had moved to New Orleans five years earlier along with my aunt Annett. They later persuaded my mother to move after telling her about all the benefits she could receive on welfare with five children. When they told my mother she would receive three hundred and fifty dollars a month, it didn't take much persuading after that.

After visiting my sister Katy in Detroit for a couple of weeks after graduation, I decided to move to Washington, DC, where my sister Selenia lived. Selenia had gotten married the summer before we moved to New Orleans to an airman in the air force named Richard Johnson. He was stationed at Andrews Air Force Base. They eloped so none of my family knew much about Richard, but he and my sister invited me to come and live with them and attend Howard University. I arrived in Washington, DC, in June of 1972 on a Greyhound bus, and my life would never be normal as most people call normal again. Selenia and Richard picked me up at the bus station in their new car. I was impressed. No one in our family had ever owned a new car. I knew I was in the right place. They seemed very happy to see me, Richard had this huge smile on his face hugged me and said, "How are you, brother-in-law?" I liked him right from the start.

The bus station was in downtown Washington, DC. Richard took the scenic route home, and as we drove past the Washington Monument, the Lincoln Memorial, and many of the historical buildings, it hit me that we were in the nation's capital. All the things I had read about in my history books I was experiencing firsthand, and it was a wonderful feeling. We stopped at KFC and got something to eat before arriving at their apartment in Anna Costa. It was getting dark, so I couldn't see much, but it looked like a very nice place. After eating KFC and all the fixings, I was tired and needed to lie down. Richard showed me where I would be sleeping, and as soon as my head hit the pillow, I was asleep. Later that night, I was awakened by the sound of Marvin Gaye's music and what sounded like a party. I opened the door and walked down the hallway and was greeted by about twenty people all drinking and dancing and having a good time.

My sister said, shouting over the music, "Hey, everybody, this is my brother from New Orleans. He's going to be staying with us. He is big for his age. He's only eighteen, so don't none of you fast-assed women start getting any ideas!" I was six feet tall at eighteen and thought I had it going on, especially with the ladies. As I looked around the room, I noticed most of their friends were women and three or four men including Richard. I learned through their conversations that after college, they all came to DC to work for the government. Everybody began to say hello as they welcomed me to DC. One of Richard's friends, Carl Hayes, came over to talk to me. He called me "youngblood" and began telling me about himself. He was cool, but I thought he talked too much. I later learned one of the ladies I had my eyes on was with Carl. He introduced me to her. Her name was Teresa. They were getting ready to leave the party when out of the blue, he suggested that he would come by on Monday and show me around DC. As everyone began to leave the party, my sister asked me to walk two of her friends to their apartment two buildings away. I happily said I would. They introduced themselves as Thelma and Sharon, and they flirted with me all the way to their apartment, but they weren't serious, so I thought. They invited me in.

"Make yourself at home," they said as they walked into separate rooms. Sharon came out of her room first wearing a robe and asked if I wanted something to drink, and I said sure. I thought she meant soda or water. She poured a glass of wine and handed it to me. I acted like it was cool, but I had never had alcohol before. I sat down on the sofa, and before I could taste my first sip of wine, the phone rang. It was Selenia.

I could hear her loud and clear. "You fast-assed hussies, send my brother home right now!" I could hear her laughing as I jumped off the sofa and headed for the door.

My first week in Washington was lots of fun. Hayes picked me up on Monday and showed me around DC, stopping by many of his friends' apartments and introducing me as his buddy. After a couple days of hanging together, Hayes and I became friends. He was a few years older than me, but he didn't act any older. We had a lot of fun hanging out together, but I needed to make some money before I started school. The next week, I went to work with my sister Selenia. Selenia worked as a collections agent at a furniture store called Heckman's on H. Street Southeast. There were stores on both sides of the street for miles, and I was feeling confident about finding a job as we got off the bus. I said good-bye to Selenia and started walking. I soon learned finding a job was not going to be as easy as I thought. After walking into about thirty stores and filling out twenty applications, it was lunch time. I saw a F. W. Woolworth across the street and decided to have lunch there. I sat down at the counter and ordered a burger, fries, and a root beer. I saw this guy sitting next to me with his foot in a cast and crutches beside his chair. He noticed that I was staring at him and asked, "What's your name, youngblood?"

I said, "Johnny."

"Speak up," he said.

"Johnny," I said in a loud voice.

"Everybody calls me Bass, Jim Bass. What's your game," he asked.

I said, "I don't have a game."

"Sure you do. Everybody has a game," he said. "What do you do?" he asked.

"I don't do anything. I am looking for a job to make some money before I start school. I am going to Howard in the fall."

"What can you do?" he asked.

"Just about anything I guess," I replied.

"Can you sell?" he asked.

"Sell what?" I said.

"When you finish your burger, come down two blocks on the left-hand side to Bernard's Men's Clothing and talk to me. I may have a job for you." I was so excited! Mr. Bass grabbed his crutches and hopped out the door. I ate my burger and fries as fast as I could, and out the door I went. After talking to me for a few minutes, Mr. Bass gave me a job as a salesman. He introduced me to one of his salesmen named Smitty. He said, "Watch Smitty. He will teach you how to sell. He's my best salesman." Smitty put me to work right away. I did all the things he was supposed to be doing. It was okay. I was just happy to have a job. After working with Smitty for a few hours, I came to the conclusion that Smitty was a nice guy and fun to be around. Everybody called me Youngblood. I asked Smitty what it meant. He said it meant I was still wet behind the ears.

I called my sister and told her I found a job and was working. When I told her where, she said, "Put Mr. Bass on the phone."

I told Mr. Bass, "Telephone. My sister wants to speak with you." When I gave him the phone, he said hello and started laughing loudly; he and my sister knew each other and thought it was quite a coincidence that he was the one who had given me a job. I felt comfortable knowing she knew Mr. Bass, and after one week, everyone concluded I was a natural-born salesman. It just came natural to me; I loved clothes and loved to sell them to people. After three weeks on the job, Smitty was no longer top salesman. Mr. Bass was always bragging to everyone about how good a salesman I was. The word got around to some of the other store owners, and they started coming by Bernard's Men's Clothing to watch me sell. I didn't understand. To me, it was nothing special; it came natural. Jerry Reese, who owned House of Jerry's on Fourteenth Street, and Larry Natham, the owner of Mr. Men's downtown, came by. Smitty told me every salesman in town wanted to work at Mr. Men's. It was the number one men's and women's store in DC. Smitty explained to me that they never had openings for salesman at Mr. Men's because no one ever left. It was my third week on the job, a Saturday, when Mr. Bass asked me if I wanted to play my number. I asked him to explain the numbers to me. He explained that for every dollar, I play. I win if the number hits, and I get $550. Pick three numbers and place your bet," he said. I chose 726 for ten dollars. I remembered when my Greyhound bus pulled into Washington, DC. It was 7:26. Mr. Bass laughed at me and walked away.

That Monday, when I came to work and walked in the front door, everyone got quiet. Then Smitty shouted, "Your number hit straight 726." Mr. Bass laughed and said I was the luckiest man he ever met. He took me in the back office and counted out $5,500 in hundred-dollar bills. It was more money than I had ever seen at one time in my life, and it was all mine." I called my sister and told her what happened, and it was like she was standing outside the door to Bernard's Place. That is how fast she got to the store. I gave her $500 for herself and asked her if I could buy a car.

She said, "It's your money, and you can do anything you want with it." The next day, Mr. Bass took me to the Buick Dealership owned by his friend. I bought a brand new Electra 225, the sticker price was $6,300, and he sold it to me for $5,500. Mr. Bass told me to put $4,000 down and put the other $1,000 in the bank. The next day, Mr. Bass took me to DMV. He went inside and got a study book and told me to study it; as I read through it, he was telling me the answers. After thirty minutes, he said, "Go take the test. You can pass." When I came out of the DMV with my learner's permit, Mr. Bass looked at me, shook his head, and said, "I knew you were lucky. I don't know anyone that does that." I thought he did. I think, that is why I passed.

I got my license one week later, along with my insurance. I picked up my new car. I knew how to drive. I had been driving every chance I got without my license. Now I was happy to have my license. I stopped by the music store and bought an eight-track tape of the Chi-Lites, let the sun roof back, and drove around DC.

Mr. Men's

I felt like I was on top of the world as I cruised around downtown. I passed Mr. Men's and decided to take a look inside. The first thing I noticed was the windows with all the beautiful clothes, shoes from $85 to $125, suits from $250 to $300. This store was top of the line, and the clothes were much more expensive than what we were selling at Bernard's Men's Clothing. I went inside the store, and it was beautiful. The fixtures were hardwood and brass with beautiful carpet on the floor. All the salesmen were dressed in suits and ties and looked well groomed. I was impressed. "Can I help you?" one of the salesmen asked.

"No. I am just looking around," I said. As I looked around, I was amazed at how beautiful the store was and said to myself, "A black man owns this store." While I was looking around, a young man came into the store inquiring about a suit in the window. The salesman told him they were sold out and would have more in about a week to ten days. I looked at the young man and estimated his size to be size 40 regular, which is the size of most mannequins used in window displays. I said to the salesman the one in the window could be his size. He asked him his size, and he was a 40 regular.

They took the suit out of the window, and it fit him perfectly. He bought the suit, shirt, and tie. All together, it was a $375 sale. Mr. Natham was watching from his office and came down the steps and called his entire sales staff and introduced me.

"Remember I told you that he could sell sand on the beach." He had come back to his store and told his salesmen he had just seen a natural-born salesman; I was bursting with pride. Mr. Natham introduced me to his wife, Zoie. She took me by the hand and started to walk and talk. I know what Bernard pays his salesmen. She said, "Come work for us and you could double your salary." Before I knew it, I had said yes. I asked if I could start in about ten days; I wanted to give Mr. Bass a week's notice. She shook my hand and said, "We will do the paperwork when you report to work." I looked around to see where Mr. Natham was. He was sitting in a chair with his legs crossed, smiling. I walked outside and looked back at the store and was excited about working there. I needed new clothes. I didn't own clothes like what his salesmen wore. I got into my new car only to find a ticket on the windshield for ten dollars.

Now I had to tell Mr. Bass I had accepted another job. I felt loyalty to Mr. Bass because had given me my first job. As I was parking in front of the store after a long lunch break, Smitty came out of the store, and then Mr. Bass came out also to see my car. Then Bernard, Mr. Bass's partner, came out the door. It was my first time meeting Bernard. He had been vacationing in Florida for three weeks at his condo where he played golf. He was much younger looking than Mr. Bass, and the clothes he wore we didn't sell at Bernard's. So this is the young man you have been telling me about as he shook my hand. I noticed he wore wire-rimmed glasses I learned they were made of real gold and wore a huge diamond ring on his little finger, which I later learned were called pinky rings. Parked across the street was a new Cadillac Eldorado, yellow with a white top that belonged to Bernard. One glance at Bernard and you could tell he was rich. We all went inside as more customers walked into the store. I was not as happy as I could have been. I still needed to tell Mr. Bass about my new job at Mr. Men's. Later that afternoon, Mr. Bass came over and put his arms around me and said, "Larry called and told me he offered you a job, and you accepted. I think you would like working for Larry Natham. He's a good brother," Mr. Bass said. He will teach you the clothing business, and one day you can have your own store. Work the rest of the week and take a few days off before you start your new job. Boy, that took a load off my shoulders. I had never experienced knowing people that wanted you to get ahead without thinking about themselves. Before I left Bernard's Men's Clothing, I hit the number again *the same number*. Mr. Bass had taught me to box my number, that means any way the number came, I win. It was 276; three dollars boxed paid me $1,650. I put a thousand in the bank, took the balance, and bought clothes for my new job. I was meeting a few nice ladies and thought I needed my own apartment. I talked to Selenia about moving into my own apartment, and she didn't seem to object to the idea. She agreed we would look for an apartment on her days off. She would have to sign for me to get it. The apartment I chose was six blocks from my new job. It was a brand new twelve-story high rise at 1234 Massachusetts Avenue. Selenia thought the monthly rent of $350 for a one bedroom was more than I could afford, but I convinced her that I would be okay. I also convinced her, my mother, and my sister Katy to allow me to skip the first semester of school and start in the spring. Katy was firmly against the idea; she told me that most people who put off going to college never complete their education. I convinced her this would not happen to me. I wanted Katy to come and visit me in Washington when she could. I wanted to see her and show her my new apartment and my new car. Katy and her husband were having marital problems and had separated; she needed a break from Detroit and her husband. She made plans to come in about two weeks, and it is now thirteen years later as I begin to tell the story of *Methadone* to my sister Katy as she lay in her bed dying from cancer. She wanted to know what had happened to me in Washington that distanced me from our family during my time there. I sat by her bed for five days and told her the story that changed my life forever.

Doc and Katy Visit Washington, DC

"It all started when you came to visit me in Washington, DC," I said to Katy. "You and Rick had separated and were waiting for your divorce to become final. You came to visit with your friend Dr. Michael. He was a very interesting man, and we got along as if we had known each other for years. The way he talked to me made me feel like I was an old friend. I called him Doc after getting his permission. I was excited to see you and show you my new apartment. I was working at Mr. Men's clothing store. Doc told me he was having problems finding clothes with any style in the big and tall stores in Detroit. Doc was 6'8," and weighed about 260 pounds. He asked if I could help. I told him I sure could and would give him a call when I had some clothes I though he may like. I asked Doc how much he wanted to spend. He responded that there was no limit. He wanted to change his complete wardrobe for summer and fall. That was exciting; I knew that would be a good commission for me! After two months at Mr. Men's, I was promoted to store manager. Mr. Natham said he liked my style and began teaching me all he could about the clothing business, just as Mr. Bass had said. At the menswear show in New York, I ordered Doc a complete wardrobe—suits, shirts, shoes and pants—all totaled to about five thousand dollars. When the shipment came in, I called Doc and gave him the good news. He sounded excited and couldn't wait to see what I had for him. He told me he would be in DC in about two days. Two days later, I picked Doc up at the airport and took him straight to the store. Doc liked everything I had purchased for him and everything fit with a little help from our tailor. Doc pulled out his American Express, his bill was five thousand six hundred dollars, and he added five hundred dollars to his bill, a tip for me. It was the largest tip and the largest sale we had ever made at one time in the store. Doc asked me to ship the clothes to him once the alterations were completed. Doc and I went to lunch, and afterward, I took him to his hotel. "The same place you and he stayed when you came to visit," I told Katy, "the Hilton." During lunch, we had an interesting conversation. He told me about his medical practice in Detroit, stating that he owned four family medical clinics and lots of other things. But what he said next would change my life forever. He began telling me stories about his family.

"You know," he said, "there is no Mafia in Detroit. We are the only city in the country that is not mafia controlled. You know why? My family wouldn't let them in. My family controls organized crime in the city of Detroit. The numbers played in all the auto plants in Detroit are controlled by my family. It is my city. If you ever need anything and I mean *anything*, give me a call." I tried to act cool like I knew what he was talking about, but I knew one thing: he was clearly out of my league. I knew about the numbers, but *organized crime*? I was not quite sure what that meant. The next morning, I picked Doc up at his hotel and took him to the airport. We said good-bye, and as he walked away, he looked back and said, "*Don't* forget what we talked about." I shook my head as to say I won't. How could I? That's all I had thought about all night long. When I arrived at the store that morning, Mr. Natham could not wait to talk. Mr. Natham, the owner and his wife, Zoie, were from Raleigh, NC. As the story goes, he was related to the Isley Brothers. Mr. Natham had one of the finest men's and women's clothing stores in Washington, DC. Everybody that was anybody shopped at his store. He himself was a very sharp dresser, who wore three-piece suit most of the time. Everything he wore always matched perfectly. Shoes, socks, tie, shirt, suit—all looked as if they were tailor-made just for him. He and his wife, Zoie, were top socialites in DC, class from A to Z.

"Tell me about Doc…Where did you meet him?" Mr. Natham asked.

"I met Doc when my sister Katy came to visit me. He was impressed with the way I dressed and asked if I could help him with his wardrobe. I told him I would, and he gave me an open checkbook." Mr. Natham was impressed and reached in his jacket pocket and gave me an envelope with five one hundred dollar bills in it, the tip Doc had put on his American Express card. Brenda, the manager of Mr. Men's for Her and the best sales person in her department, came over to congratulate me on the sale. Brenda worked for Mr. Men's for Her for five years. The store had fourteen sales people all in all. I had less seniority than any of them, but I was the one promoted to manager and buyer. Every morning, when Mr. Natham arrived at the store, I was waiting for him at the front door. I was never late. Whenever he had a question about anything, I always seemed to have the answer. I think my promotion came when we had fifty thousand dollars tied up in summer suits that were tying up our line of credit with our suppliers. I suggested to Mr. Natham that we put an ad in the paper: "Buy one suit get the second one for half price." This would free up the cash we had invested in summer suits that were not moving, Mr. Natham agreed, and we sold every suit in stock in two weeks. We also attracted new customers that came in the store for the first time to take advantage of the sale. Mr. Natham was a happy man! After that suggestion, I was Mr. Natham's right-hand man. He overlooked my age and went with his gut feeling. Within six weeks, I was promoted to general manager. We made a good team, Mr. Natham and I, and the store was doing very well. After living in Washington for four months, things were going very well. It was Saturday evening around five, and the store closed at six. I asked Mr. Natham if I could get off early. I wanted to get ready for happy hour, so I could arrive early at a hot club called the Fox Trap. I had five hundred dollars in my pocket and was planning on having a nice time. I called my girlfriend Simone and invited her to meet me at the club. She said yes. I met Simone while working at the store. She was beautiful and a junior at Howard University. In DC, women outnumbered the men, eight to one, Men were given lots of choices when it came to women. I chose Simone. There was no question in my mind Washington was the right place for me. There was a group of young people in DC that were always invited to the hip parties and social events; without trying to be a part of that group, I had become a part of that group. I was invited to all the hip functions. I had a lot of friends. Some I met while living with my sister Selenia and her husband Richard. Most of my other friends I met while working at Mr. Men's, and Bernard's Clothing. "You were upset with me when I did not register for the fall semester at Howard and told you that I was putting school off," I said to Katy. "But I assured you that I would register the next semester. I was making very good money at Mr. Men's, and I had developed a lifestyle that required me to continue to make money. If I went to college, I would have to move back with my sister Selenia." And the thought of that was not appealing to me.

Lewis

Happy hour started at five. I arrived at the club around seven. The place was getting packed. My friends Sherman and Lynwood were seated at a table and had already attracted two very beautiful young ladies. I sat down and ordered two bottles of champagne, twenty five dollars each. After that, all the ladies had their eyes on our table. Champagne always got the lady's attention. I noticed Brenda from the store seated at a table in the corner with three guys that I had not seen before. Tina and Myra, two of Brenda's friends, were seated with them. These guys were well dressed with lots of jewelry on. In DC, we called these type of guys high rollers, and they were also drinking champagne. Brenda spotted me looking toward their table and waved. I waved back as to say hello. Brenda knew a lot of beautiful women in DC. That is how Simone and I had met. Brenda introduced us. Brenda always attracted high rollers, but I couldn't get these guys Brenda was with out of my mind. I had met plenty high rollers before that came through the store, but it was something about these guys that was different. Brenda and her party were leaving the club, and on her way out, she stopped by our table and introduced her friends, "Hey, guys, I want you to meet my friends," she said. "This is Lewis, Fred, and Sherman." We said hello and introduced ourselves. Brenda said they were headed to another club and then out to dinner at Anna Maria's, an Italian restaurant that I loved. She asked if we wanted to join them. I told Brenda I was waiting for Simone and we would meet them there later. I guess the reason I had this weird feeling about Brenda's friends is because they would play a major part in the way my life would take a drastic turn. Simone finally showed up looking stunning as usual. I had not seen her in a few days and could not wait to be alone with her. She was hot and dressed to impress as always.

We left the club later and decided to go to Anna Maria's. And sure enough, Brenda and her crew were there and had secured a large enough table for everyone. They were already having drinks and shrimp cocktail appetizers. I introduced Simone to Brenda's friends, and as we sat down, the waiter arrived with another bottle of champagne, and Lewis quickly ordered another. I was beginning to like this guy. Most high rollers in Washington were pretending. To me, he seemed to be one of those who were not pretending. After a few drinks, we began to joke and have fun, talking about what was going on in DC, sports, politics, and the way we talked. Lewis and his crew had a southern accent mixed with a proper northern tone, of course. I had tried very hard to change my southern accent and worked very hard to us proper English. We all ordered dinner. I always ordered the same thing, eggplant parmesan. As we ordered, two men dressed in suits walked into the restaurant and ordered coffee to go. The presence of the two men changed the dispositions of Lewis and his crew. The men stared at our table as they waited for their coffee. Dinner could not come fast enough for Lewis, Fred, and Sherman. They wanted to get out of there as soon as possible. The rest of the group at the table except Lynwood and I didn't think much of the change in the attitude of these guys, but I was always curious and noticed every detail. We finished dinner, which happened very fast, and Lewis threw two one hundred dollar bills on the table, and he and his crew were out the door! Simone and I said good-bye to my crew and headed to my apartment. We started making love in the elevator. We could not wait! When we made love, we could feel each other's soul. We made love on and off throughout the night as we had done many times before.

"You did not have to tell me all that," Katy said, but I wanted her to understand my mind-set during my whole experience in DC. My great grandmother was full-blooded Cherokee Indian and would always say it made our blood run hot. I got up the next morning and made pancakes. Neither of us had to work or go to school; it was Sunday. So we had breakfast in bed and watched TV. The phone rang, and it was Brenda inviting us to dinner at Lewis's house. I told Brenda I wasn't sure of our plans. But when she gave me the address, it did pique my curiosity. The house was located in Rock Creek Park, an exclusive part of DC. I watched football, and Simone studied for an exam. Later that afternoon, we both were getting hungry and decided to take Brenda up on the invitation. We got dressed. Simone called Brenda, and we were on our way. She told us there was plenty of food and fun so we should hurry up. When we arrived, there were at least twenty cars parked in the driveway and along the street. It looked like a party was going on! When Brenda answered the door, she had an apron on and greeted us with a drink in her hand. Hellos came from everywhere. Lynwood and Sherman were sitting on the couch, and the smell of marijuana was throughout the house. The Spinners were playing on the stereo. This was a typical '70s party. But what was not typical was the amount of marijuana and cocaine that was everywhere you looked; bowls were set out for people to use freely. Cocaine was expensive, and nobody gave it away, at least not the people we knew. Simone and I were very hungry, so we headed for the food. There was a spread of down-home cooking, chicken, ham, pork chops, ribs, and all the fixings, and the food was delicious. Fred walked up to Simone and me and asked how the food was. We told him how wonderful it was, and we were surprised when he said he cooked everything. He told us he was a chef for four- and five-star hotels for years. After eating, Simone and I were invited to another room where Lewis and

Brenda were. This was a huge bedroom with people I had never met sitting on the bed and on the floor smoking marijuana and snorting cocaine. Lewis asked us to join the party. I sat down and joined in the conversation about politics, the upcoming election, the state of affairs, and women and their shopping. As they passed the bowl of cocaine and marijuana around, I noticed when it got to Lewis, he passed it on without using any, and when it got to me, I did the same. I had no problem with what other people did or didn't do, but I had no use for drugs. I got up, went back into the living room. and sat down. Lewis followed shortly. He was very friendly and began to open up to me. He told me he owned two restaurants in Greenville, South Carolina, his hometown and was planning to open a couple in DC; that made everything fit together with Fred being a chef. He told me that Brenda had told him I was the manager at Mr. Men's and that he was looking forward to visiting the store and checking out our clothing. I assured him he would not be disappointed. It was getting late. I found Simone, said good-bye, and left. Simone said she was not comfortable around all the drugs and was surprised at the people she and I knew who used drugs. I took Simone home, kissed her good-bye, and headed to my apartment. Monday was a workday and was harder than any other day. I crashed early. The next morning at the store, Brenda asked me if I had a good time. "Yes," I replied, "the food was great," and I thanked her for inviting Simon and me.

Mr. Natham and I headed upstairs for our usual Monday morning meeting where we would discuss sales from the week before and what stock was coming in that week and what we needed to order. We had added a new line of shoes from Italy that were selling great. Reorders took at least three weeks, so we had to anticipate what was going to sell in color and size trying not to lose any sales. The house comptroller and CPA Bill Tillis would come and join the meeting to talk numbers, which were always good and surpassed projections. I headed back downstairs to meet with our sales staff to talk about our goals for the week. Mr. Natham came down later. He and I headed out for breakfast, and as always, everyone started hollering out what they wanted, and as always we ignored them and kept on walking. Mr. Natham and I loved to check out our competitor's windows after breakfast, as we walked back toward the store. We talked about the upcoming New York menswear show, which he, his wife Zoie, and I would attend, and the show in Paris, which he and Zoie always attended. When we got back to the store, it was filled with excitement. Lewis had arrived with about seven people in his entourage. All of them I'd met the day before at his party. They were all picking out clothes like there was no tomorrow. Mr. Natham asked me if I knew these guys, and I told him they were friends of Brenda, and I had met them over the weekend at a party. I told Mr. Natham that Lewis owned two restaurants in South Carolina and was looking at opening some in DC. About that time, Brenda came over and introduced Lewis to Mr. Natham. Lewis told Mr Natham he loved the store and the clothes. He told Mr. Natham he had seen clothing stores like ours in New York, but he was not aware of any in DC. I told Lewis to feel free to ask if I could assist with anything. When Lewis and the guys had completed their shopping spree, they had spent over twelve thousand dollars and change. Mr. Natham was so excited. I think he went upstairs and had a drink of that fifteen-year-old Scotch he had in his office. With that sale, we reached half of our projection for the week. What a sale... and they paid in cash! Lewis sat down and began to talk about his love for the store. I told him about the famous clients we had and discussed the pictures of some of them on our wall of fame. He joked and said he needed to be added to the wall. At least I thought it was a joke. None of the guys wanted alterations they had their own tailors. That was great because to complete all the alterations would have cost the store at least five hundred dollars. It was a great day. Mr. Natham went home early and asked me to close the store that evening. After closing, I headed home. I needed some rest and decided not to go out that night. When I walked in the door, the phone rang, and it was Doc. I had not heard from him since he purchased his new wardrobe. He sounded excited. He had some friends that loved his new clothes and wanted to schedule a time in the near future to bring them to DC to shop at the store. I told Doc that was great, to get with the guys and determine a date so I would make myself available. Doc said, "We will see you in two weeks, and if the date changes I will give you a call." He asked how I was doing and if I needed anything. I said no, thanked him in advance for bringing the guys down, and hung up. At Mr. Men's, business had increased in every department. "Everything was going great." Brenda seemed to have struck it rich. She was spending money and doing things she never did before…like buying lunch for everybody. I knew she was dating Lewis, but I was a little concerned. Brenda was sharp but a little naïve about some things, but she was a big girl and seemed to know what she was doing. About one week after, Lewis and I met. I arrived home, and my phone rang. It was Brenda, and she wanted to come by. She said Lewis had a proposition I could be interested in. I said come over in about thirty minutes. In the building I lived in at 1234 Massachusetts Avenue, guests had to check in at the front desk before being allowed to come up to your apartment. I called the desk and informed Denise I was expecting guests. The doorbell rang I opened the door and expecting to see Brenda and Lewis, and instead, Lewis was alone. He said he wanted to speak to me alone. Brenda was waiting in the car downstairs.

"Have a seat. What's on your mind?" I said.

"Boy," he said, "you get right to the point!"

I smiled and asked if he wanted something to drink. "What do you have? Hard or soft?" he asked.

"I'll take Rum and Coke, if you have it." I fixed the drinks and sat down on the sofa across from Lewis.

"How much do you make at Mr. Men's," he asked?

"About twenty-two thousand dollars a year," I was proud to say. In 1972, that was very good pay.

"How would you like to make ten thousand dollars more per year?" he said. "I like Mr. Men's. It's a great concept. I would like to open a store just like Mr. Men's in Georgetown. How much do you think it would cost to turnkey the project?"

I said, "About one million with stock. Mr. Natham had discussed with me his loan with the SBA and when he expected the loan to be repaid."

"I will put up the one million," Lewis said, "if you come on board. Brenda has already agreed. I will give you ten thousand dollars today if you say yes. Brenda, I only gave five thousand dollars. So, is it a deal?" Now I knew where Brenda got the money she was spending like water.

"Lewis, it sounds too good to turn down, but I am going to have to say no. You see, Mr. Natham is my boss, but he is also my friend, and I don't want him to feel betrayed by a friend, not by me. Although I would have more money, it would never feel right to me, you understand?"

Lewis looked at me and smiled and said, "Guys like you are hard to find. You see, although I have the money, it didn't feel right to me either. When you are in business, your feelings grow cold, and it has a lot to do with the people you do business with." Lewis and I talked for about three hours. He told me it was very seldom you meet people you can feel relaxed around. He thought my apartment was a great place to relax. Brenda had called to inform him she had to make some runs and to call her when he was ready to leave. I told Lewis I would take him home when he was ready to leave. I took Lewis home around midnight. The next day was my day off. Whenever I worked on Saturday, I got a day off during the week. Lewis and I hung out together most of the day. I took Lewis to the driving range. He had never played golf and wanted to learn. Mr Natham was teaching me, and it had become my passion. After hitting golf balls, we decided to have lunch in Georgetown. I thought I saw the same car and the same two guys everywhere we went. I mentioned it to Lewis, and it didn't seem to bother him at all that I thought we were being followed. Maybe I was imagining it all. I took Lewis home, and when we pulled in the driveway, Fred and Sherman were waiting. They seemed very anxious. When Lewis got out of my car, they all got into their car quickly, sped off as if there was a fire they were going to put out. I tried not to think about it, but I knew it was more to Lewis and his crew than restaurants. I began to wonder about Lewis and all the money he had. To acquire that type of money, he was either doing something wrong, maybe his family was wealthy, or someone had died and left him a bunch of money. I wanted to think the best of Lewis. He seemed like a nice guy. He looked and dressed like a businessman. I never asked his age, but I guess twenty five or twenty six. I had met quite a few young men in DC who were doing very well for themselves. "My gut feeling was telling me this was different."

I drove home and parked my car in the underground parking garage and took the elevator to the lobby. Harry, the attendant, told me I had company; it was Simone. I had not seen her for three days because she was taking final exams, and this was a great surprise. When she opened the door, she greeted me wearing only a G-string and nothing else. ("There you go again," Katy said). She turned around and walked toward the bedroom without looking back. When I walked into the bedroom, she pushed me on the bed and walked over to the stereo and put on Marvin Gaye's "Let's get it on" and danced the entire song. I was about to explode!. She jumped on top of me and began taking my clothes off...She wouldn't allow me to help. When she took off my pants, I could see the excitement in her eyes as she saw I was about to explode. ("Boy, when did you get so mannish," Katy said...I smiled and continued to talk as she blushed.) I could not take it anymore. I grabbed Simone, threw her on the bed, and we made love for hours without saying anything at all. The next morning,

I left for work, and Simone stayed at the apartment. I gave her keys to the car in case she wanted to hang out. When I walked into Mr. Men's, the place was quiet when I said good morning to everyone. They treated me like Judas. Mr. Natham asked to see me in his office, and his wife, Zoie, followed us upstairs. I was wondering what was going on. When he spoke, it became clear. Brenda, hoping to save her job by putting her spin on Lewis's proposition, told Mr. Natham I was teaming up with Lewis to open a store in Georgetown and tried to recruit her. I was angry, but I didn't want Brenda to lose her job. I told Mr. Natham it was true Lewis had offered me a job with a ten thousand-dollar raise but that I turned him down. I told Lewis there could be only one Mr. Men's, and that you and I were more than employee and employer; we were friends, and friends don't betray friends.

Zoie looked at Mr. Natham and said, "I told you it was nothing, and you got me all upset with Johnny for nothing. We love you, baby," she said and kissed me on the cheek and told Mr. Natham to give me the raise they had discussed. Instead of losing my job, I got a one-hundred-dollar-a-week raise, and Brenda still had her job. When Mr. Natham and I came down the stairs smiling and hugging shoulder-to-shoulder, the whole store came alive again, and you could see the smiles on the employees' faces. The rest of the day, Brenda did everything she could to avoid me, which was fine with me as I was not ready to talk to her yet. When I got home that evening, there was a note from Simone. She had taken the car and hooked up with some of her friends and gone cruising. I checked the answering machine. There was a message from Doc; he was coming to town as planned and was bringing four friends. This was exciting. This could be a huge sales week for the store, and I was thinking what a great day it had turned out to be. At that moment, the intercom rang from the front desk. I had a visitor; it was Brenda. I told the desk to send her up. I was not expecting her to be ready to talk so soon, but I knew she wanted to find out what I had told Mr. Natham. I knew she wanted to find out why she had not been fired. She walked in the door and asked if I had company. I said no; then she started to explain and apologized for what she had done and wanted to know what I had told Mr. Natham. I told her exactly what I told Mr. Natham; and I had not implicated her in any way. She thanked me and tried to kiss me; but I turned away.

Brenda said to me, "I know you want some of this," running her hands the complete length of my body.

"I do," I said, but I want Simone more, and she would never forgive me if I did. Plus I told her she was Lewis's girl, and Brenda stated that Lewis and I are just friends, and Lewis had plenty of girls in ten different cities.

"How do you know that?" I asked. I know more than he thinks I know, and you should be careful hanging out with him if you know what's good for you. "Brenda," I said, "tell me what you mean," and she just turned and walked out the door. After all that drama though, finally I could relax and reflect on the day's events. Afterward, I laid on the sofa to watch some TV. After a short while, the TV was watching me.

The Gang Arrested

I woke to the sound of the door opening. Only Simone and Mr. Bass had keys to my apartment. I was expecting Simone, but it was Mr. Bass. Mr. Bass and I had stayed in touch since my days at Bernard's Men's Clothing. He always gave me good advice whenever I needed to talk to someone older. He was carrying a newspaper, the *Evening Post*. "Did you hear about the huge drug bust? It was all over the news."

"No," I said. "I slept through the *Evening News*. At that moment, the phone rang. It was Brenda.

"Did you see the news?" she asked, all excited.

"Let me call you back," I said and hung up the phone. Then Bass opened the paper, and there it was the picture of about ten men and two ladies. The headlines read, "Largest Drug Bust in DEA History." Mr. Bass asked if these were the guys I was telling him about. I took a good look at the paper, and sure enough, it was Fred and Sherman and some of the other guys I saw at the party. But there was no picture of Lewis.

"Yes," I told him, "these were the guys."

Mr. Bass said, "These guys are heavyweights. Look at the amount of drugs they were moving." I read the article, and it stated they had been investigating this drug ring for two years, and the investigation covered seven states and fourteen cities. They had seized over two and a half million dollars and one hundred kilos of heroin.

The phone rang. It was Mr. Natham. "Did you see the news?" he asked. "It seemed everybody had seen the news or read the paper."

"Yes," I said. "Mr. Natham, can I call you back? I am reading the article." I continued to read the article as Mr. Bass fixed a drink and offered me one. I think I said yes twice. The paper went on to state that the ring had been smuggling drugs from Vietnam, and the investigation could involve others. Mr. Bass wanted to know more about how I knew them. I said Lewis and I were becoming friends, and I only met the other guys through Lewis. Lewis said he owed restaurants in Greenville, South Carolina, and was looking to open some in DC. There was no picture of Lewis in the paper. Mr Bass said he's probably running and that they will catch him sooner or later. I asked Mr. Bass if he thought I was in trouble. I told him about the time Lewis and I were in Georgetown and how I thought we were being followed. He said I probably didn't have anything to worry about. They surely knew everyone involved. That made me feel better.

The phone rang again. It was Brenda. She didn't wait for me to call back and said she really needed someone to talk to. She blurted out, "I told you to stay away from those guys," and continued to tell me all she had seen. Mr. Bass told me to tell her to be quiet and stop talking over the phone. I quickly understood what he was saying and told Brenda to be quiet and we would talk tomorrow. Mr. Bass wanted to know everything I knew about the guys, which was not much. Lewis never had reason to discuss any of his business with me. Mr. Bass finished his drink and said good-bye. I needed Simone. I needed someone to talk to that I could trust. I laid across the bed and tried to imagine what Lewis was going through on the run, what it must feel like. I quickly fell asleep and woke up the next morning and couldn't wait to get to work and get other opinions about what was happening. When I opened the store, Brenda was the first to arrive at work. She was nervous and had the same question for me that I asked Mr. Bass.

"Johnny, do you think they think I am involved?" I wanted to play a joke on her and tell her they may pick her up for questioning, but I decided not to and told her what Mr. Bass had told me. After two years of investigation, they knew everyone involved. She was putting cream and sugar in her coffee and was shaking so hard that the coffee was falling on the floor. The rest of the staff began coming in with the morning papers under their arms. I asked Jimmy, one of the salesmen, if there was anything in the paper about the drug bust. He said yes and handed me the paper. As I read it, there was very little new information, except they gave some background on some of the people involved; but there was nothing about Lewis. I thought it very peculiar that Brenda had not asked about Lewis, like where he may be hiding. Okay, maybe she was just nervous, and it was too much for her to handle, too much to comprehend. Mr. Natham came in through the back door, and I was the first person he saw.

"They were good customers while they lasted," he said, smiling with newspaper under his arm. (Katy thought that was funny and laughed so hard she started coughing and couldn't stop. The nurse came in and asked me to leave, for she needed her rest. Katy didn't want me to stop. She wanted me to continue. I convinced her we could start where I left off on tomorrow. When I arrived the next day she knew the exact word I said, and I started from there).

After about thirty minutes Mr. Natham and I headed out for breakfast as we always did. He wanted to know the same thing Mr. Bass wanted to know, how I knew these guys. I gave him the same answer I gave Mr. Bass: Lewis and I had spent some time together, the other guys I only saw in his company. I did tell him about the last time Lewis and I were together and how they left his home in a big hurry when I dropped him off. I said there is no mention of Lewis in the article. Mr. Natham's remarks were the same as Mr. Bass's: he is probably on the run. I told Mr. Natham, Doc was coming to town and was bringing four of his friends to buy new wardrobes. He smiled and said that was the great news for the day. We got back to the store, and Simone was there talking to Brenda. She seemed to be concentrating on something Brenda was telling her. They stopped talking as I got near. Simone said hello and gave me a kiss and asked if I would take her home. She was still driving my car. While I was driving Simone home, she said she thought something was going on with Brenda and tried to get her to tell her what was wrong, but she wouldn't say. I reassured Simone that Brenda was just nervous about what was going on with Lewis. She told me she felt it was more than that but wouldn't comment further. I dropped Simone at her home and headed to my apartment to change clothes and pick up my golf clubs. Mr. Natham asked me if I wanted to play a round when I got back, which sounded great to me. Mr. Natham had taught me the game of golf, and I loved to play. When I got to my apartment, Bobby, who was managing the front desk, said he had a package for me. I told him I would have to pick it up later that afternoon because he was busy with two others, and I didn't have time to wait. My mother was always sending me food by mail: baked cakes, homemade gumbo, and, one time, a baked duck with cornbread dressing. She was the best cook in the world. I assumed the package was from her, and it could wait…I had a tee time to make! When I picked Mr. Natham up, he was waiting at the front door. We played eighteen holes. I was getting better but no match for Mr. Natham. He was a six handicap, and some days he played better than that. I dropped Mr. Natham at the store after our round, and he told me he would close and I could take the evening off. I parked my car, removed my clubs, and headed for the elevator. I stepped off the elevator into the lobby with my hands full. Bobby, who was still on duty, reminded me of the package he had for me. He told me the package was rather large. Seeing that my hands were full, he offered to send it up later. I opened my door and found balloons attached to a card. It was from Simone, and it was the first time I can remember she said she loved me and how I made her feel. It felt good to have someone who loved you, but at this point in my life, for some reason, I thought everything was temporary and love sounded long-term. The doorbell rang, I knew it was my package and opened my door. When I saw Davis, the maintenance man, with the package on the hand truck, I wondered what it was and who it was from. He placed the box in the middle of the living room. I gave him a tip, and he left. The name and return address were not familiar. My first thought was that Simone had ordered something for me and it was a surprise. I opened the box only to find a piece of luggage the size of a carry-on bag made of leather, real nice leather. I lifted the luggage out of the box. It was heavy it was full of something. As I lifted it out, an envelope fell out from the bottom. I opened it as fast as I could and started to read it. It was from Lewis. The note read: "You are the only one I can trust at this time. I have only known you for a short period of time, but I know I can trust you. If you could keep this package for me, I would greatly appreciate it. I will be in touch. Thanks." There was something else in the envelope, a key. All I could think about was this thing was full of drugs and how much trouble I could be in! I opened the case slowly, and to my surprise, it was full of cash, hundred dollar bills from top to bottom. There was another note just a plain piece of paper folded in half. It read three and one half million, give or take a few thousand. I sat back on the sofa to catch my breath. This was too much for me to digest. I just sat quietly on the sofa and tried to take it all in. I sat there looking at all that money, and I noticed a velvet bag. I moved a couple stacks of money to get a better look. I had seen this kind of bag before. It was a Crown Royal bag with the gold string, and there was another envelope underneath the bag with my name one it. I opened the bag and poured the contents on the sofa: gold rings watches and all kind of jewelry in diamonds and gold. There was more jewelry in it than in a jewelry store. I got up from the sofa with the envelope in my hand, went over to the bar, and fixed myself a drink. By this time, I was sweating like I did in the cotton fields in Mississippi on a hot summer day!

"Oh, Lord, what was I to do? I didn't ask to be put in this position, and neither was I given a choice." I sat at the bar and again found myself staring at the sofa now littered with gold, diamonds, and jewelry. I realized I still had the envelope in my hand with my name on it. I opened it, and there were two stacks of hundred dollar bills about two inches thick. I counted it twice. It was twenty five thousand dollars. I had been taught all my life: you work hard, and you would be rewarded and blessed in the end. Ever since I have been in Washington, money has been falling out of the sky. Now I have twenty five thousand dollars. It's more money than I make in a year, three and half million, and I don't know what to do with it. Until I figure what to do with the money, I have to find some place to put it. I put the jewelry back in the case, closed it shut. "For now, I'll put it in my closet." I knew if I told anyone about the money, my life would be in danger, people in DC were being killed for a whole lot less, and I knew I couldn't keep it in my apartment. I tried to sit still but found myself pacing the floor, back and forth. Then I decided what to do. The building had a storage facility on the top floor that was available to every tenant. People in DC who worked for the government would leave for months at a time and would put their things in storage and keep them there until they returned. Anyone could get storage free of charge. There were all different sizes, and you could choose the size you needed, and you had your own lock. I called the front desk and asked to speak to Dave the maintenance man, and he called me back. I told him what I needed. He said no problem and explained the process. He took me up to the storage area where I could choose the size I needed. He would assign me the storage, and I would sign for it. I chose a four by eight, the smallest they had. Dave asked if I needed a lock. They were six dollars each. I gave him six dollars, and he came back with a lock still in the package. I was all set. I went back to my apartment, put the case back in the box, and took it to storage. The box looked out of place, sitting there all alone. I looked around, and there were some empty boxes in the corner, so I took them and put them in the storage. The boxes were a little dusty, which made them look like they had been in storage a long time, which was good. I put the lock on it.

When I got back to my apartment, I took the twenty five thousand dollars and laid across the bed and fell asleep. I heard the doorbell ring and wondered how someone could come up to my apartment without being announced. I looked through the peep hole and saw three men dressed in suits. They shouted, "FBI! We would like to talk to you! Open up!" I opened the door, and the men pushed their way into my apartment and pushed me onto the sofa and started yelling, "Where is Lewis, and where is the money?" Before I could say anything, one of them pulled out a gun and pointed it at my head and pulled the trigger. The gun sounded like a cannon it was the loudest sound I had ever heard. I was sweating all over, and then I woke up. What a dream! I looked at the clock. It was 2:00 a.m. I still had my clothes on and $25,000 in my hand. I put the money in my closet; then I took a shower and dressed for bed. I couldn't go back to sleep. I kept thinking about the dream and the position Lewis had put me in. Then I started thinking about crazy things like what if he gets killed, what if he goes to jail, what if what if. I finally fell asleep. I woke up the next morning, hoping it was a bad dream. I looked into the closet, and there was the $25,000, still in the brown envelope where I had placed it. When I opened my bank account with McGlocklyn National Bank, they gave me a free safety deposit box. I decided to go by the bank before work and put the $25,000 in my box. I got dressed for work, and before leaving the building, I took a trip up to the storage just to make sure everything was okay. Everything was just as I left it. I walked to the bank, which was four blocks from Mr. Men's. It felt like everyone I passed knew I had the money and could see in my jacket pocket. I guess it is safe to say I was a little paranoid. When I arrived at the bank, the teller assigned me a safety deposit box and showed me how to access it. She took my box and put it in a private room about the size of a cubicle and instructed me how to replace it when I was finished. I put $23,000 in the box, took $2,000, and bought six money orders for $300 each and $200 in my pocket.

(Katy said, "I can't believe you kept the money."

"Of course I did! Remember when the pastor we had at our church in Mississippi, Bishop Patterson, who said the wealth of the sinners was laid up for the just. I think I remember that sermon more than any others. When he said that, I was thirteen years old. Proverbs 13:22. I must have read that a hundred times when I got home from church.

Katy smiled and said, "You would remember that, of all things." We laughed and she said to go on.)

When I got to work, I mailed a money order to my mother and all five sisters. It felt great sending them the money. I knew they could use it. When Mr. Natham and Zoie arrived at work, Mr. Natham asked me to take a buying trip with his wife, Zoie, one week from today. I said sure. I loved going on buying trips to New York. Most of the time, it was me and Mr. Natham. This was the first trip Zoie and I would take together. We would always leave early, about 8:00 a.m., arrive in New York around noon, have lunch and work the garment district until 6:00 or 7:00 p.m., then have dinner with some of Mr. Natham's and Zoie's friends. After dinner, we would have drinks, talk about what we had bought, then go back to the hotel. We would get up around 9:00 a.m., have breakfast, shop until around 2:00 p.m., and leave before rush hour. The day before the trip, I left early from work. Having taken the company car home, I picked Mrs. Natham up at 7:45 a.m., and we were on our way. The conversation was lighthearted. Zoie talked about the spring show in Paris she and Mr. Natham always attended each year and how she was looking forward to the upcoming trip. She wanted to know if I was happy living in Washington and working at the store. I told her I was very happy. If I could express my happiness, I would jump out of the car and run the rest of the way to New York. She thought that was funny. We arrived in New York on time, and everything went according to plan. We had lunch and began work. I learned we were there looking for miniskirts. Zoie had not bought enough at the spring show, and we needed enough to last through the holiday season. After visiting some design houses, Zoie only chose three styles that she really loved, and we called it a day. Zoie had four more design houses we would visit the next morning. That evening, we had dinner at this great chop house with Carl and Kermit, two of Zoie's friends. They had two friends with them. One was Ms. Barbara Simmons, a beautiful woman who reminded me of Zoie, very elegant with lots of class, and she looked to be in her early thirties. She kept flirting with me all evening. Carl and Kermit were business partners in a beautiful clothing store on the Upper East Side. They were also life partners. Their other friend's name was Teddy. I was not sure where he fit into this equation, but he sat next to Zoie. The food was great, the best steak I ever had! After dinner, Zoie invited them all back to our hotel for drinks. When we got to the hotel, I said good night. I was tired from the very long day we had. When I got to my room, I called Simone to tell her I was in New York. Normally when I travel out of town, she would stay in my apartment. But after the dream I had, I did not feel safe with her being there. She knew I was in New York because she had called the store and talked to Brenda. She tells everything. She even knew when I would be back. We talked on the phone for about an hour. I was starting to miss her. We had not been together for a few days. I hung up the phone and jumped in and out of the shower and was ready for bed. I had been waiting for this moment for hours. I climbed into bed turned on the TV and began to relax when someone knocked at the door. I jumped up from the bed and put my pants on. I assumed it was Zoie. Her room was on the same floor, and she probably wanted to discuss the itinerary for the next day, but why didn't she call? I opened the door, and my heart skipped a beat. It was Lewis. He had a big smile on his face and asked if I was going to invite him in. I said, "Sure. Come on in. How did you know I was here?"

"I talked to Brenda," he said. I knew it! She had stayed in touch with Lewis. I knew when I saw her talking to Simone, and they got quiet when I approached them in the store. Somehow, I knew they were talking about Lewis. I asked Lewis how he was doing. "Fine," he said. "If you ever want to get lost, come to New York. Fidel Castro could come here every week and shop, and no one would ever pay him any attention. I needed to lay low for a while, could not think of a better place. But things have cooled off a bit, according to the attorneys. None of the guys they took into custody gave me up. I surrounded myself with real men and knew they would never talk. The guys I question I never let them close enough to have anything on me. Plus I needed to be on the outside to take care of their families and attorney fees. Those blood-sucking attorneys, when they know it is a drug case, try to take you for every dime. It cost me $250,000 cash, and there seems to be no end in sight. They already asked me to bring another $150,000. That's $400,000. At this rate I could run out of money quick, and that's not including the money I sent to wives and girlfriends. You can't believe the lifestyle they try to maintain." I am sitting there wondering why is he telling me all this. The less I know, the better, but I looked as if I were all ears. "I got to start making money quick," Lewis said, "or I could run dry. I have ten cities that are turning a hundred keys every thirty days. That's two and a half million dollars every thirty days, and the network is still in place. If I don't put these people to work soon, I am going to lose them and the network to someone else." It was amazing to hear him speak. He talked like an employer running a company like it was legal.

"I have the money you sent me. What do you want me to do with it and when do you want to pick it up," I said.

"That's cop money. It has to stay out of the mix, if you don't mind holding on to it for a little longer."

That was more choices than I had at first! I thought.

Lewis said, "I got a meeting. I'll be in touch. I hope the money I gave you was worth the trouble I put you through. Maybe I can add a little more."

I said, "No, you don't have to do that. I would have done it for free."

"I know. That is why I left it with you." He walked to door and let himself out. After Lewis left, I wondered why all this was happening to me, how had I gotten myself involved. I laid back on the bed and tried to digest what had just happened. For some reason, I thought about the money. The amount of money he was making was mind-boggling to say the least. A knock at my door. "What did he forget? Could it be the police coming to arrest me?"

They knocked again, I opened the door. It was Barbara Simmons, Zoie's friend from dinner. She said the same thing Lewis did, "Are you going to let me in?" Before I could say yes, she was in the door and sitting in the chair next to the bed. "Were you asleep?" she asked.

"No, I was watching TV. Would you like some company?"

"I have a girlfriend," I said.

"Boy, where did that come from I thought!"

I know it sounded immature.

"I have a man friend," she said. "But tonight, I want all he has to belong to you. Can you handle that? Does that make you happy?" As she was talking she was taking her clothes off. I watched her take off one piece at a time until there was nothing left but her bra and thong panties and high heels. She looked like a track star. Her calves and thighs were firm, and her breast were twice the size of Simone's.

(Katy said, "Johnny, you can skip that part."

I said, "No, in order for you to understand how I changed, you need to know every detail of what happened to me.")

This was a real woman. She walked toward me, and the next thing I knew my male hormones took over, and she was in my arms and on the bed, but she was not having any of it. She made it clear she was directing the show. She was the star. She told me everything she wanted me to do to her. Every action I took slowed down to a snail's pace when I touched where she wanted me to. I could feel her body tremble, and she would moan with pleasure; then she would tell me something else to do. That night, I explored parts of a woman's body like never before and went places I never thought I was supposed to go. She gave every part of her body to me, and at the right time, she made me explode. This show she directed lasted about an hour and a half, and then it was over. I felt totally drained and feel asleep in her arms like a little baby. When I woke up the next morning, Barbara was gone. The only sign she had been there was her perfume. I showered and got dressed and met Zoie downstairs for breakfast. She had a smile on her face and asked me if I had slept well. It sounded like a normal question, but I knew it wasn't. We finished breakfast and hit three designer houses, completing our buying trip. I picked up two miniskirts for Simone, and we were on the road. When we passed through the Harlem Tunnel on our way home, I felt as if I were leaving something behind. I couldn't get Barbara out of my mind. I thought Simone and I made love, but in comparison, it was puppy love. Zoie saw me smiling, looked at me, smiled, and said, "The word you are looking for is *turned out*."

"Turned out," I said. Zoie said yes. It is when an older woman takes a younger man and shows him how to please a woman. She smiled, and I knew I had been setup, but why? Zoie told me Barbara would be in DC in about two weeks and would love to see me again. That was exciting, but why didn't she tell me? I just had a visit from Lewis, and none of that mattered. My thoughts were on Barbara. We arrived at the store about five in the evening, one hour before the store closed, and unloaded the collection of miniskirts. Steve, our stock man, inventoried them and put them out before we left.

"How was the trip?" Mr. Natham asked.

"It was great!" I parked the car in the garage and said good-bye and walked to my apartment.

I went inside and got the storage key and checked on the money. Everything was just as I had left it. I went back down to my apartment and checked the answering machine. Doc had called, and he was coming to DC in two days and wanted me to call him if that was not a good time. I quickly called him. He always seemed to be happy when I called. We talked for a while about his trip to DC. He always asked how I was doing as if he really cared. It always feels nice to know that someone cares. I wondered if it was because of the relationship he had with you, Katy. I felt we were becoming close, maybe good friends. The other calls were from Mr. Bass, Lynwood, and Sherman. Bass's call sounded urgent, so I called him back first.

"Where have you been? I went up to New York for a few days. Tell me about the dream you had about the Bishop," he asked. (The Bishop was a prophet that traveled to different cities each week and held meetings. People would come and pack the places he rented just to hear him speak about God, and in the end, he would give them the number.) Mr. Bass and I had gone with him on one trip to Newark, New Jersey, and were amazed at the people that would show up to hear him prophesy. I had dreamed that Bishop was shot and killed and had told Mr. Bass.

"His wife shot and killed him yesterday," Bass said.

"What happened," I asked. He was pistol-whipping her, and the gun slipped out of his hand, and she shot him dead."

"What!"

"I told Smitty you had dreamed about it two weeks ago." I could hear Smitty in the background telling Mr. Bass to tell me not to have any dreams about him, unless I dreamed he hit the number. We both laughed.

"I'll call you about the funeral arrangements." I couldn't believe it. Bishop is gone. He was a strange bird, wore tailor-made suits, had a chauffer-driven Cadillac, and had a German Shepherd named Satan. Mr. Bass said the dog snorted cocaine and was a junkie. I got undressed and was trying to decide if I wanted to go out with Lynwood and Sherman. That was what they were calling about. I decided to stay home and chill. So much had happened in the last couple of days, and I just wanted to digest it all. I took a shower and decided to watch TV and pay some monthly bills. I was not ready to see Simone, but I knew she wanted to see me, at least I thought she did. After a while, I fell asleep on the sofa. I heard the phone ring, and I thought I was dreaming. After I realized I wasn't, I answered the phone.

It was you, Katy. It was good to hear your voice. I had not spoken to you in two weeks. As always you wanted to know how I was doing, then you answered your own question by saying, "You must be doing okay. I received the money you sent. I talked to Mamma and the rest of the crew, and they all received checks. Mamma wants to know where you are getting all this money from. Selenia said you hit the number or something like that."

"Yes," I said, and after I told you how the numbers worked, you seemed to be okay. You began to tell me about every member of our family and how they were doing. Your son Cedric was having problems in public school, and you wanted to send him to a Catholic school a few blocks from your home, but it cost $7,000 a year. You had to pay half, and the state would pay the other half. I knew you were not telling me this thinking I may be able to help, because you always told me everything that was going on with you. I said to you, "So you need $3,500?"

"Yes," you said slowly.

"I have some number money left. I can send you the money." It was as if the phone went dead, so I said, "Hello, hello."

"I am still here," you said.

"Did you say you had the money?"

"Yes, I will send it tomorrow," and you started praising the Lord and said you would pay me back. I knew you would never be able to pay me back, so I went along with you knowing it would make you feel better. We said our good-byes and hung up the phone. I went back to sleep.

I woke up and looked at the clock, and it was 11:25. I had been asleep for four hours. I wondered why I had not heard from Simone. I knew she knew I was home. My thinking was crazy. I didn't want to talk to her, but I was concerned she had not called. "Get a grip," I told myself as I hung the miniskirts for her in the closet. I felt refreshed and decided to go join Lynwood and Sherman for a few hours. I knew the way we club-hopped. By now, they were at our second spot, Larry Browns. I had to go past the Fox Trap on the way to Larry Browns, so I decided to swing by and see if I saw Sherman's car. This place was always crowded; people were outside standing, cars letting people out and picking people up. As I turned the corner, still caught up in the traffic, I saw Simone coming out of the club holding hands with another guy. I questioned my eyes and quickly said to myself, "That's not Simone," but it was! They got into a car parked three cars in front of me. He opened the door and let her in and went to the other side. When he got in, Simone slid over to get closer to him. I had seen him before. He was older than our crew—well dressed and always had a younger woman with him. Just as I edged closer, the car in front of me let their car pull out in front of theirs. I was devastated! I could not believe what I had just seen. I knew the dating code in DC was that you had a main squeeze and maybe one or two on the side, but I thought Simone and I had something different. I never questioned her love for me; I didn't feel much like clubbing after that and went home. I pulled my car into the garage and sat there in a trance. A horn blew. It was my neighbor John saying hello. I threw up my hand to say hello, got out of my car, and went up to my apartment. I sat on my couch and cried for the first time in my life over the first woman I cared about. Then I thought about the fact that the night before I was making love to a complete stranger who changed the way I felt about making love to a woman, so much so that I didn't know if I wanted to see Simone until that feeling faded. Was that the reason this happened to me? Was it payback? I looked at the clock it was twelve thirty. I pulled my clothes off and crawled into bed. I laid on my back staring at the ceiling until I drifted off to sleep, only to be awakened by kisses on my face. I opened my eyes. It was Simone. I looked at my watch before I said hello. It was 3:30 a.m. She smiled and asked when did I get home. She caught me by surprise. I had no time to think about what I would do or would say to her. I just said, "I saw you tonight." She looked deep into my eyes got up from the side of the bed and went over and sat in the chair. She didn't ask where or make excuses. She began to tell me about him.

"His name is Ron Styles. I met him my freshman year at Howard. I don't love him. He is my benefactor. Some would call him my sugar daddy. He pays my bills, helps with my tuition, and asks very little from me in return. Yes, we have sex together, and yes we had sex tonight. If you do not want to see me again I understand, but I love you," she said. After silence that seemed like an hour, she got up and walked toward the door. I grabbed her by the arm. I could not let her walk out the door. For some reason, she was more attractive to me than she had ever been. I was impressed with how honest she was. I pulled her on to the bed beside me, and we lay quiet for about an hour. After that, she got up, pulled her clothes off, and got into the bed. I don't think we said another thing the entire evening. I got up the next morning and got dressed for work. Simone hugged me and told me how much she loved me, and she decided to stay in the apartment and cook dinner for me. She had never cooked for me before. That was a surprise. I didn't even know she could cook. I got to work, and Mr. Natham and I went through our morning routine. We talked about Doc and his friends coming in the next day and what we needed to do to get ready for their visit. After our meeting, Brenda tried everything she could to find out if I had seen Lewis in New York or how much I really knew about what was going on. I made a decision, that whatever happened between Lewis and I, Brenda would be the last to know. I learned from experience she was not trustworthy. Besides I was sure she knew about Simone's sugar daddy.

The Deal

Doc's visit was all the talk among the salesmen. They remembered the last time he came, and every salesman wanted a piece of the action. Mr. Natham decided to have a drawing, allowing two more salesmen to assist Mr. Natham and me with Doc and his friends. Mr. Brady and Jimmy won the drawing. The others were disappointed, but what they didn't know was that Mr. Natham and I had decided to split our sales with the whole menswear sales staff. About three o'clock in the afternoon, I was sitting alone in the lounge reading *Women's Wear Daily* magazine when Brenda made one last attempt to see if I would give her any information. I was sure she had stayed in touch with Lewis, but I was somewhat sure she had not seen him. She wanted me to say I had seen him so she could pursue the questions she needed answered. She started the conversation about Doc's visit and the miniskirts Zoie and I had bought in New York. Then she said, "I heard you had a visitor in New York." At that point I knew she had talked to Lewis and he had told her that we talked, but I was not going to confirm I had talked to anyone. I learned from church as a boy that by two or more witnesses, something is confirmed.

"Yes, meeting Zoie and Mr. Natham's friends was great, and we had a great time." She looked at me, dropped her bottom lip and walked away. We received the shipment of dresses Zoie had been talking about since her trip to Paris. She was very excited that they had arrived. They were beautiful and pricey, four styles and six different colors. Zoie had ordered three sizes in each style and color but in size eight. There were only two of each style and color. Zoie asked Steve to bring her the invoice. Sure enough, the invoice stated they had shipped three in size eight, but they were not there. Steve admitted he didn't really check and just assumed they were all there. Zoie asked Steve to fill out a claim ticket to be sent to the manufacturer. Mr. Natham didn't buy Steve's story and walked away without saying a word. Steve followed behind him trying to convince him the shipment was short. Mr. Natham went out the back door where the company garage was located. I assumed he was leaving for the day, but a few minutes later, he came in the door with the dresses. When Mr. Natham came back in the store with the dresses, Steve ran out the front door without looking back. Mr. Natham said he knew the dresses had been stolen when the missing lots were all the same size. Steve's wife was size eight. He was stealing dresses for his wife. Only God knows how much other stuff Steve had stolen. He had worked for Mr. Men's for three years, and no one really checked behind him. What Mr. Natham did next surprised me and everyone else. He said it was my fault not Steve's. I should have had a system in place to prevent this from happening. I saw disappointment in Mr. Natham's eyes for the first time. I knew he was fond of Steve. Mr. Natham and Zoie left, and I closed the store and walked home. When I arrived home, I didn't remember the walk. I was thinking about people you think you can trust and think you know, and then you realize you really don't know them at all. Right then, I came up with a system of knowing people in layers. There is a surface layer they want you to know, and there's another layer that belongs to them, and always, the layers of sin are exposed.

I could not wait to see what Simone had cooked. I opened the door and saw quickly Simone was not there. I looked on the stove and could not believe my eyes. Mac and cheese, cabbage, cornbread, yams and fried chicken and a note from Simone telling me she had to run to her dorm and would be back soon with a "PS: I have your car." The food was still warm, that let me know she had not been gone long. I washed my hands and started fixing me a plate, not before grabbing a chicken leg and giving it a sample. The front desk called to let me know I had company. Simone had called Lynwood, Mr. Bass, Hayes, and Sherman and invited them over. Lynwood and I worked together, and he never let me know he was invited. Simone wanted to surprise me. The food was great, and the company even better. Everyone raved about how good the food was, and just like me, they couldn't believe Simone had cooked it. The phone rang. It was Doc. He heard the noise and asked if it was having a party. I told him what was happening and how good the food was. He said he wished he were there. He was calling to let me know that his plane would be arriving late on Friday and leaving early on Saturday morning. He wanted to know if we would keep the store open late to take care of him and his party. After the stop in DC, they were headed to Las Vegas on a chartered private jet sent for him and his friends from Las Vegas. I was impressed and told him I was sure it would not be a problem. I hung up and called Mr. Natham to make the new arrangements, and as I expected, it was no problem. After good food and a couple of drinks, the guys were ready to leave. Simone came in just in time to receive the accolades for what was a great evening. As the guys were leaving, Mr. Bass told me the Bishop's funeral was taking place Saturday at 2:00 p.m. I assured him I would be there. Simone started right on the dishes, and the whole scene reminded me of someone who was married. It was obvious she wanted to please me and make me happy. But I could not help but wonder where this "domestic woman" had been all through our relationship the three months. We sat on the couch and had a drink, and one thing led to another, and we were in the bedroom making love. I decided I wanted to try what happened to me in New York with Barbara on Simone. She allowed me to enter all the places Barbara had me to explore with her body. I was amazed. The reaction was the same. Simone looked at me like she was making love to a complete stranger. It lasted about the same as with Barbara, one and a half hours, and we were drained. This time it was Simone who crawled up into my arms like a baby and fell asleep. The next morning, Simone was up before me getting dressed. Before she said good morning, her words were "Where did that come from? You took our love making to another level. I am not complaining, but who have you been giving this kind of loving to, and why me now?" I remembered what Zoie told me as we were driving back from New York. You don't make love, real love to someone unless you are sure you want to keep them around. I couldn't tell Simone the truth. I smiled and walked into the shower giving myself a chance to think. I was not ready for what came out of her mouth next. "I think we should live together," she said. "Think about it, and we can talk about it later." She kissed me and rushed out to class. Bass jokingly made the comment during dinner that when a woman starts showing her skills, she is getting serious, whether you are serious or not. I got dressed and headed to work. Mr. Natham came in around noon. And I had already told the salesmen, that would be helping with Doc and his party, that they would be working late. That evening, Doc arrived in a chauffer-driven limo with a party of six instead of four. Doc had two women with him. Brenda was about to leave and decided to stay. Doc was wearing one of the outfits I sold him earlier, and he looked sharp. Doc introduced his party as the men started looking around. Once we saw their sizes, we were putting outfits together as fast as they could try them on, and Brenda was working on the women. The men trusted our choices of outfits and offered very little resistance. We were very good at determining a person's style by what they were wearing. What we were not sure of was if they were buying all the outfits they were trying on or if they were going to choose what they wanted once they were finished. They bought it all. One of Doc's friends said the one outfit he had on he wanted to take to Vegas and wanted to know if it could be ready. That started a flood of requests for outfits they wanted to take to Vegas. Mr. Natham asked me to run up to the bus stop and see if Jed, our tailor, was there and if I would bring him back to the store. Thank God. Jed was just about to step onto the bus when I called his name. I told him what was going on, and he was more than willing to help. He just needed a ride home later. I assured him that was no problem. Everyone was happy when I walked in the door with Jed. He started taking measurements. Each salesman had his customer's clothes separated as Mr. Natham started adding the totals. After three hours, Doc's party had spent more than fifteen thousand dollars, and the women were still shopping! Doc asked if Mr. Natham would like to go out to dinner with him and his party. Mr. Natham stayed behind and made sure everything was ready when they returned, but insisted I go. Doc had reservations at the Golden Palace, the finest Chinese restaurant in DC. They called ahead and ordered duck, which took hours to prepare. One thing about Doc is, he seemed to know how to have fun, and it appeared that money was not a concern. They placed us in a private room, and it was obvious Doc had been there before and had left a good impression. The food was great. I had tried Chinese food before, but some of the dishes they ordered I had never tried. I tried to remember the names because I knew I wanted to try them again. They talked about the Vegas trip, who won and who lost on previous trips, and how they planned to take the house, whatever that meant. From the conversation, I learned two of Doc's friends were doctors, and the others were lawyers, and the two very good-looking women were along for the ride. One of the ladies had just finished a billboard shoot for Canadian Mist, some kind of Canadian whiskey. One of Doc's friends picked up the check, and another left a tip of one hundred dollars. The owner escorted our party to the door, welcoming us back soon. The limo pulled up as we walked out of the restaurant, and the door opened before we reached the limo. We arrived back at the store to find everything they were taking with them boxed and ready to go. Brenda informed me the ladies clothes had not been paid for. I informed Doc, and with one motion, he pulled out his American Express and paid the $1,500 bill with no questions asked and gave the staff a tip of $1,000 to share. The plane was leaving the next morning. Doc pulled me aside, and again he asked how I was doing and if I needed anything. I Informed Doc I was fine and thanked him for all he had done; and then for some reason I wanted to tell Doc about the conversation I had with Lewis in New York.

"Doc," I said, "there is something I would like to discuss with you, but I don't want to delay you any longer. I will talk to you later." Without saying a word, Doc turned and walked to the limo spoke to the driver, and it pulled off and Doc walked back toward me.

"The driver will be back in an hour. Let's walk across the street and have something to drink." I had no idea this conversation would change the course of history for my life and many others forever. I asked Doc if he had heard about the big drug bust that was all over the national news about a month ago. He was very much aware of it. He knew every detail. I told Doc how I met Lewis and the conversation we had in New York. After I finished talking, Doc commented it would be a shame to let that network dry up; then he said he could fill the void, but he would only go through me. I don't want to meet him ever.

I said, "Doc, I don't know anything about drugs. I know it's deadly. I read about it in the paper all the time, people getting killed for little or nothing when it relates to drugs."

"Don't worry," he said. "I will keep you safe, and I will keep you clean." For some reason, I felt he could and would. Doc told me exactly how to frame my conversation with Lewis. "Never mention my name or the city where I live, and never let the conversation include me in the third person." Doc leaned in very close and said, "Now this is what you tell your boy. It will cost him $25,000 a key. It will be the same quality or better guaranteed, and he can get as much as he can afford. For you, I will give you $2,000 for every key he buys, and that's between you and me, and you never touch anything but your money. Make it happen." We got up from the table. He paid the bill, and we walked out of the door where his driver was waiting. He said, "I will call you later." On my way home my mind was turning a thousand miles a minute. Lewis was moving a hundred kilos every thirty days, and that was $200,000 for me, and that's a lot of money. I knew in my heart if I crossed this line, I could never go back. My mother raised six children, and none of them had ever been arrested or in trouble for anything. We were brought up in a Christian home and were taught the golden rules from an early age, but something excited me and frightened me at the same time. I looked over at Katy and saw the disappointed look on her face; she knew the choice I made. I knew Lewis had not found a place to buy because I still had the cop money. Even if I decided to move forward, I needed to get in touch with Lewis, and the only way to do that was to put my trust in Brenda and I was not about to do that. I finally reached my apartment and was relieved Simone was not there. I needed to be alone. This was a decision I needed some advice on, but I knew this was one decision I had to make alone: if I crossed this bridge, no one could ever know. I took a long shower and lay in bed with my hands behind my head, staring at the ceiling as always when I had a decision I had to make. Remembering I had not checked my answering machine, I quickly got up and turned it on...(....Selenia and you, Katy, had called...).... With all that was happening I forgot to send the money, I promised. There was a message from Bass reminding me of Bishop's funeral, and a message from Barbara in New York, just calling to say hello and to let me know that she was thinking about me. How did she get this number? Zoie must have given it to her. I started feeling her all over again as if we had just made love an hour ago. I played the message over again just to hear her voice. She had not given me her number, so I had no way of calling her back. I went back to the bedroom much happier than I came out. Just the idea she was thinking about me made me feel connected to her.

The Funeral

By the time my head hit the pillow, I was out, and morning came quickly. It was Saturday my scheduled day off. The phone rang. It was Mr. Natham. He was still excited about the sale last night and wanted me to know he would not be in the store. He would be playing golf with friends. He knew it was my day off but wanted to know if I would meet Isaac Hayes who was a customer of ours coming in about four thirty. He always liked Mr. Natham or Sandra to take care of him. Mr. Natham wanted to make sure Mr. Hayes was well taken care of. I told him I had to attend a funeral at two but would be at the store before four. After finding out who he was playing with, I told him to hit them straight and hung up. I was not looking forward to the Bishop's funeral. It would be the first funeral I attended as an adult. I attended my great grandmother's funeral when I was eight, and that was it. I arrived about thirty minutes early. Bass asked me to get there early to meet him at the entrance so we could sit together. I turned onto G Street and was shocked there were cars parked on both sides of the street, police directing traffic and people walking along the sidewalk. There were seven black limos lined up behind the hearse. I was not expecting such a large turnout for the Bishop. I located a parking space three blocks away. Walking back to the church I noticed cars with license tags from ten different states. Finally I saw Mr. Bass and Bernard waiting outside. They waved me through the crowd, Smitty was holding our seats. Mr. Bass said we should hurry before they have two funerals; the Bishop's and Smitty's. The church was packed and people were standing against the wall, there were no seats. I saw Bishop's wife sitting on the front row with Bishop's shepherd and the dog had on a tuxedo. I pointed that out to Bass and Bernard, they both laughed and said Bishop loved that dog. I opened the program and read the names of the speakers and they were from Chicago, Philadelphia, Detroit, and even as far as Los Angeles. The funeral started on time with a song I remembered from my days as a youth in church, "Going up a yonder to be with my Lord." The choir started singing, Bishop's wife started crying loud, and the dog started howling, and before you knew it, before the song was over, there was not a dry eye in the place! Bishop's obituary stated that he was affiliated with the United House of Prayer for All People, started by Charles M. "Sweet Daddy" Grace in the early 1900s. I had no idea who that was until Mr. Bass told me after the service. The preacher that spoke on behalf of Bishop and his family was very charismatic and kept saying Bishop was not dead but was alive walking around the church, taking names of all who attended.

Smitty leaned over and whispered into Mr. Bass's ear and said, "I am glad I came. I would hate for Bishop not to have me on his list!" (Katy started to laugh and cough, and I knew it was time to stop. "I will be back tomorrow. Get some rest." She didn't want me to stop, but I insisted. I arrived the next day and again she knew where I had stopped.)

The service lasted about an hour, and they rolled Bishop's casket out the front door, and there was at least three hundred people waiting outside of the church. Mr. Bass and Bernard and I stood outside talking about what a nice homegoing Bishop had, and I said to Bernard, "I thought you were playing golf with Mr. Natham."

He looked at me and said, "I am, if anyone asks you."

There goes the layers again, I thought. Even Mr. Natham has them. I arrived at the store about 4:15 p.m., hoping I was not late for Mr. Hayes only to find out he had changed plans and would be coming in the next week.

I noticed Zoie sitting alone in the lounge area and headed over to say hello, and before I could, she said, "I gave Barbara your number. I didn't think you would mind."

"No, it was nice to hear from her. I was not home when she called, so she left a message on the answering machine." I asked Zoie how was business.

"Okay, but nothing like last night," she said smiling. I smiled, said good-bye to everyone, and made my exit. I had the weekend off, money in my pocket, and could do anything I wanted, but for some reason, I felt I had unfinished business I needed to take care of. I knew Doc would be calling in a day or so to see where our deal stood with Lewis. I needed to talk to Lewis, and conveying that to Brenda was not an option. I needed to find Lewis on my own. I had recently met an older guy in my building that always had encouraging words for me. I later learned his name was Petey Greene. Shortly after I got to my apartment, the doorbell rang. I wondered who it could be. Simone and Bass had keys. They would not be ringing the bell. I looked through the peephole, and it was Mr. Greene. I opened the door, and he came in acting like we were good friends and had known each other forever. He looked around the apartment and commented on how nicely it was decorated. He sat down and asked if I had something to drink...

"Hard liquor preferably," he said. I fixed him a drink, turned the TV on, and we watched sports together. After a few drinks, he began talking about his children and his ex-wife and began to cry. I was only eighteen and could not offer any advice, but I don't think he wanted any. I think he just wanted me to listen. After a few more drinks, he got up and walked out the door. "See you later, Youngblood," and that would not be his last visit. I laid on the bed thinking about Bishop's funeral and all that happened today and decided to nap. I had barely fallen asleep when the fire alarm went off in the building, and we all had to evacuate. As we all stood in the parking lot waiting for the firemen to arrive, I realized it was the first time I had seen most of the tenants who lived in my building. It was quite a diverse group. As the fireman arrived and rushed up the stairs, all of us were very concerned about our belongings and me, all the money I knew was in my storage.

Someone whispered in my ear and said, "It's that damned Petey Greene trying to cook again. He does this every time he gets drunk and tries to cook!" At that moment, I felt responsible for Mr. Green. I had given him the drinks. Thirty minutes later, we were allowed back into the building. By this time, I was ready for bed. Forget a nap! Before I could fall asleep, Doc called.

I was not expecting his call so soon; his only words were "Have you spoken to your friend?"

"No, I haven't any way of reaching him, but I am sure I will make contact with him soon."

"Talk to you later," he said and hung up the phone. I knew Lewis had not requested his money, so I was sure he was still looking for a supplier. Finally I went to sleep. I was so happy the next day was Sunday. Watching football and being with Simone were all I wanted to do. It was two in the morning. The phone rang. It was Lewis. Before I could say his name, which was what I was about to do without thinking, he said, "Meet me tomorrow at the place we like to eat, same time," and hung up the phone. I had only eaten alone with Lewis once. We had eaten in Georgetown, and the time had to be around eleven because I had ordered breakfast. Now I couldn't sleep at all. I was wide awake. I began thinking. Did he want to make arrangements to pick up the money? Had he found a buyer? Why did he want to see me? I knew I needed to see him, but he didn't know that. Should I call Doc and let him know I had made contact? I needed to talk to someone…This was all too much for me to handle! I knew I could not talk to anyone, too dangerous. As I lay in my bed, my life began to flash before me, and I wondered how I had gotten to this point where I had to make a decision that involved right from wrong. My mother raised six children; we went to church every night and twice on Sunday. None of us had ever gone to jail or been arrested. I had never had any contact with law enforcement in any way other than a parking ticket, and now I find myself about to become a criminal in the worst way, a drug dealer. I told myself it was not too late. I can say no to Doc and give Lewis the money back, and my life would be back to normal, but there was something exciting about all of this…I can't explain…how Doc operated as a doctor and everything in between… Then there was the money; I was going to college to get a formal education to make money so I could help my family and have a better life. While I reasoned with myself one thing I knew for sure, it was wrong, and I could go to jail or be killed. I did not realize I had been awake all night as daybreak appeared through my window. I decided to move forward with the meeting. I told myself I would do it a couple of times to get enough money for college and quit. As good as it sounded, I knew I was lying to myself. I made myself feel better about doing it by telling myself, "I was not really selling drugs. I was just a middle man, and somehow my doing this was not as bad as the other drug dealers." After all, my reasons were justified. It's 6:00 a.m., and I took a shower and tried to relax before the meeting. I had not heard from Simone, and that was unusual as she called every night. I was happy she had not called because she would have been able to detect something was wrong and would not stop inquiring until I told her what it was. After my shower, I went upstairs to storage to visit the money as I did every morning and every evening. Everything was as I left it. I went back to my apartment and got dressed although it was 7:00 a.m. I put on a sweat suit, baseball cap, and sneakers. I didn't want to draw attention to how I was dressed. I always put complete thought into every outfit I put on regardless of whether it was dress or casual and always welcomed compliments. This was different. I wanted to blend in as if I were not even there. I wanted to get to the restaurant early so I could relax and look comfortable, even though I was a nervous wreck. It was only a ten-minute drive from my apartment to Georgetown, and it is nine o'clock, and I am headed down to the garage to get my car. I passed Mr. Greene in the lobby, but I was so focused on getting to my meeting with Lewis that I didn't even notice him. He really got my attention when he shouted "Hey, Youngblood, where you rushing off to?" then he said "Oh I know... going to get that money! Got to do what you got to do!" I couldn't answer or say hello... all I could think about was why he said that! Did he know something? Of course not, I was being paranoid!! Driving down Massachusetts Avenue, it was hard for me to concentrate. Everything was moving so fast! Why did Lewis choose such a public place? He was on the run. I was sure when we did meet it would be in some remote place with no one around. If this meeting goes south, my life as a drug dealer could be short-lived! I arrived at the restaurant at 10:00 a.m., only for the waiter to inform me that my party was waiting; Lewis had gotten there before me. Of course, he has more experience at this sort of thing than I do. He has probably done this a thousand times. The waiter led me to a booth located at the very back where Lewis was waiting with a huge smile on his face. He always smiled even when he talked to you, but this was different. It was as if he had already gotten the good news. He started the conversation, talking as usual, telling me things I wondered why he thought I should know, but this time, I was paying very close attention. He told me that all of his crew was out of jail on bond except Fred, and he was working hard to get him released. "Fred was the fear behind the organization. I am spending a ton of money, everything going out and nothing coming in. Even an ocean can run dry with that system." Then he said, "You needed to see me?"

I was caught off guard. I told no one, absolutely no one except Doc. How did Lewis know I needed to see him? Lewis said, "I got a phone call, and some lady told me to give Johnny a call and gave me the phone number." I didn't want him to know I was not the one who put this meeting in motion; he would have been as spooked as I was. It could have only been Doc, and at this point, I had a lot of questions for him. The waiter came over and served the coffee, and we placed our orders. When the waiter left, I asked Lewis if he had any concerns about meeting in such a public place. "No," he said. "My lawyer and I both agree for some reason they don't want me in jail, at least not yet. We are not quite sure why. If I didn't have some business to take care of in DC today, this meeting would have taken place in New York. So, what's up?"

I asked, "Are you still looking for a supplier?"

Lewis hesitated and then slowly said, "Yes." He looked at me with a look I had never seen before. I could see this game had two faces. This was the real one, and at that moment, I knew I had crossed the line of no return. "Now, are you a drug dealer?" he asked.

"No," I said. "But I have a connection. I can help if you are interested." (My answer should have been "Yes, I am a drug dealer," but I couldn't bring myself to utter the words.)

"It depends," he said. "What can you offer?"

"Okay," I said. "This is what I can tell you now. The price is $25,000 a key. The quality is the same or better than what you were getting before."

He laughed. "That could never happen. I was buying straight off the boat," he said. "If you can make that happen, set it up. How long will it take?"

I answered, "I'll get back with you with all the details."

"I will need a sample before the deal can be finalized," Lewis said.

Acting like I was totally in control, I said, "I can make that happen." When the food arrived, I was no longer hungry and got up to leave, but Lewis stopped me and said, "Eat your food. Never leave questions in someone's mind, not even a waiter's." Lewis asked me if the "package" was still intact. I assumed he was asking about the money, and I said yes. It was the first time he had asked about it.

"Lewis," I said, "you have to assure me that every conversation we have from this day forward stays between you and me."

Looking directly into my eyes with a stern, penetrating look that I had not experienced from him before and one I would never forget, he said to me, "Brother, that part is understood. That is the only lifeline we have." I had then entered into his world and that look would become one that I would become very familiar with from that day forth. After eating a few bites of our breakfast, Lewis got up from the table, looked me in the eyes, said, "Make it happen," threw a twenty-dollar bill on the table, and walked away. Those were Doc's exact words, "Make it happen." The whole time I was in the restaurant, I felt like I was suffocating. It wasn't until I got outside that I realized I was close to fainting. I left the restaurant and took a drive over to East Potomac Park, about ten minutes away. Mr. Natham and I played that golf course often, and I had grown to love the peacefulness that I felt there. The road that circled around the park had benches that you could sit on and look into the Potomac. Even though I had spent time in the park golfing, I had never taken the time to just sit there. Today, it seemed like I was just drawn back here: things were heavy on my mind, and I just needed this place and this time to get myself together and come up with a plan. I had a lot to think about. I parked my car and sat on one of the benches. I could see people playing golf, playing tennis, people walking and others just sitting as I was, staring toward the water. I knew in my heart that my soul was split that day. I felt as if a part of me had just died. I always had a sense of peace and assurance about my future. I no longer felt I was in control. One thing I knew for sure was, "For me, to survive in this game, I had to learn fast." I got back to my apartment around noon. The light was blinking on my answering machine; it was full. The first message was from Barbara. She was in town and said she couldn't wait to see me. The others were from Sherman, Cherokee, a new friend I had met at the store, and Brenda. What did she want? I turned on the TV and tried to relax and take my mind off everything that was happening, but I kept thinking about Brenda's call. "Had Lewis told her about our meeting? It would be devastating if she knew anything." I needed to know why she called. I decided to return Brenda's call.

When she answered the phone and heard my voice, her voice changed to a sarcastic tone. "Simone called me crying. She was at your apartment when she heard some woman named Barbara leaving you a message talking about she was in town and couldn't wait to see you. You men are all alike!" I asked her, why are you calling me, and not Simone?"

Calmly, I said "I will give Simone a call, Brenda. Thanks."

With an attitude, she said, "She doesn't want to talk to you now!"

"Thanks for calling, Brenda," I repeated. Now I know why I have not heard from Simone. Mr. Bass told me never give a woman the keys to your apartment. Now I know what he meant.

The Flight

Before I could give the conversation any thought, the phone rang. It was Doc. Without any greeting, he just said, "I need you to be at the airport in two hours. There will be a jet there to pick you up and bring you to Detroit. Can you make it?"

I said, "I have to work tomorrow."

He said, "You will be back in Washington before dinner. The plane will pick you up in the chartered/private plane area of Washington National Airport."

"Yes, I can make it," I said. And the phone went dead. I had never flown on a plane before. I arrived in Washington on a bus. I always wanted to fly and was planning on flying to New Orleans for Christmas. The anticipation of my meeting with Doc overrode the excitement of this being my first flight! Never would I have imagined this in my wildest dreams…I didn't even have time to be scared! As I rushed to get ready to make the flight, I thought, *I forgot to ask Doc one very important question. Why did he want to see me?*" I knew why I wanted to see him. There were so many questions I needed answered. I decided not to call Simone, knowing that would be a long conversation. I took a shower, got dressed. I had one hour to get to the airport and park. I rushed out the door. It was Sunday. At least I wouldn't have to contend with the traffic on the Fourteenth Street Bridge. I made it there with twenty minutes to spare. Signs navigated me to the chartered departure and arrival area. The chartered plane area had valet parking. I gave the attendant my keys and a five dollar tip. He gave me a stub and wished me a safe flight. I rushed into the lobby. I was there only seconds when a young lady dressed in very nice clothing approached and asked if I was Mr. Brown. I said yes.

"Follow me," she said. We walked through a tunnel with the walls lined with pictures of famous people in American history. We walked out the door, and a man took my briefcase and put it on a modified golf cart. I got on, and we headed toward the waiting plane with its engines running. I walked up the stairs of the plane. Standing at the top, a lady wearing a navy blue uniform with a red-white-and-blue-striped hat welcomed me aboard. I got onto the plane and could not help but notice how nice it was. The interior trim was mahogany wood, with white leather seats, and oriental carpet with brass trim that seemed to go on forever. There was room to seat at least fifteen people. I had nothing to compare it to since I had not flown on a plane before, but I was sure this was not the way the rest of the world was flying. In the corner sat a man dressed in a very nice suit with no expression on his face. He looked straight ahead as if I were not there. The flight attendant instructed me to sit any place I wanted. I chose the sofa-style seat, trying to act like all of this was not blowing my little country boy mind. I was only four years removed from the cotton fields of Mississippi! As soon as I was seated, the plane headed for the runway. The pilot instructed us to fasten our seatbelts and the flight attendant gave safety information, and we were on our way! I could hear the pilot talking to someone who had cleared him to takeoff. The man sitting in the corner seat, still looking straight ahead, now had his arms folded, looking like he was a permanent fixture that came with the airplane. I was surprised at how relaxed I was with flying. I was not nervous at all. It felt great. Shortly after we took off, the fasten seatbelt sign went off. A wooden door toward the front of the plane opened, and Doc walked out with a big smile on his face. I was not expecting to see him until we landed in Detroit. He greeted me with a firm handshake.

"How are things going?" he asked.

"I have a lot of questions, Doc." I said.

"I thought you might have a few, but if you hold your questions until I finish with what I have to say, some of your questions may be answered. How did your meeting go with Lewis?" That question blew my mind!

"My meeting went well. How did you know I had a meeting, and how did you get in contact with Lewis before I did?"

"Johnny, there are very few people in the US that move as much drugs as Lewis does or are doing anything else that's worth knowing about. I make it my business to know who they are and where they are. Did he accept the deal?"

"Yes, he needs a sample before he can move forward with the deal."

"Good, I will take care of the sample. Now there are some things you need to know to keep you safe and out of jail. You are going to make a lot of money, and money has accountability. You can only spend as much as you make. The accountability of your assets has to match your income, so listen carefully. On this page is everything I need you to know. Study this list, and if you have any questions when I return, I will answer them all." He handed me the paper and headed back to the door that he came out of.

"Doc, who is the guy sitting in the corner?" I whispered.

"Oh that's Nobody. Nobody goes with me everywhere I go, except to bed." Then Doc disappeared behind the wooden door. I had the feeling he was not alone behind those doors. I looked down at the paper that he gave me and was surprised to see the content. It was a dos-and-don'ts list.

Things to do:
Get a new apartment that no one knows about as soon as possible.
Keep the apartment you have.

Open a checking account; pay bills from this account.
Keep your job.

Things not to do:
Never use drugs of any kind.
Never discuss our relationship with anyone!
Never discuss with anyone what you are doing.
Don't do anything that will draw attention to yourself.

I went over the list a couple of times, some of the things I understood, but I still had some questions. After about ten minutes, Doc came in and sat very close to me looking directly into my eyes like he needed me to pay close attention to every word. He took the paper from my hand and started from the top. "You need an apartment that only you know where it is located in case you need to disappear from the rest of the world, and believe me, there will be times when you will feel the need to do so. Do not tell anyone about its location. Your life can depend on it. Second, keep your old apartment. It allows your life to flow as it has without drastic changes, which brings suspicion. Third, pay all you bills out of your checking account. Your spending should match your income in case someone is looking into your affairs. (I interrupted Doc to let him know I already had a checking account and if it was okay to use it.) Yes, fourth, you have to keep your job until we pull the plug on this operation. This is the most important thing." He continued on part two of the list. "In this business you need a clear head. You cannot do that if you use drugs, and if I find out you are using drugs, all deals between you and me end at that point! Second, keep our relationship confidential. This keeps me safe and you safe. Do not discuss with anyone what you are doing. Bragging about what you have is never a good thing. Try not to do anything that will draw attention to yourself. I cannot put more emphasis on that. For example, don't buy drinks for the whole bar. When you brought me this deal, you had concerns about safety. I told you not to be concerned. I will take care of you. These things I know will keep you safe and out of jail. You are young, and all of this is new to you, but I know this game inside and out. I know why people don't last. They end up dead or in jail. I don't want that to happen to you. I am not going to sugarcoat any of what you are about to do. It is a dangerous game. Do what I tell you, and you will have little to worry about. Now this is how this is going to work. The deal you and I made will stand. You get $2,000 for every key your man Lewis purchases. Lewis knows the price, so the only thing you will have to give him is information on how we operate. My guess is, he will purchase one hundred keys on his first buy. He needs to get his operation up and running strong and fast. My operation is a little different than most. I don't do a product and cash exchange. It is too dangerous for my people. Lewis is going to have to trust you, and you are going to have to trust me to deliver. That is a hard pill to swallow for most, but it's a take it or leave it deal. He will deliver the money, and within twenty four hours, I deliver the product. The product always matches the cash we receive at the price we set, $25,000 a key. With the network he has set up, he will probably cop every thirty to forty-five days. He will contact you when he receives the sample to let you know he is ready to move. We will let him know where to deliver the cash; it will not always be in the same place. I will rent a place for one week. Lewis will receive a key to the room. After he receives the key, he has twenty-four hours to place the money in the room. He can return in twenty-four hours, and the product will be there. It will always match the money I receive. Lewis is the only contact you will ever talk to. No one else, no exceptions! Do you understand everything I just said because we will not have this conversation again."

I said, "Yes, I understand."

He continued, "Your money will be delivered to your apartment a few days after the deal is complete. You are going to accumulate a lot of cash fast. Find a place that you think is safe, I suggest more than one. How much money do you have in the bank?"

"Two thousand five hundred dollars in checking and twenty-three thousand dollars in a safety deposit box. In the next few days, get a cashier's check from your bank and make it out to Alside Home Improvement for twenty-five hundred dollars, notes at the bottom of the check for stock purchase. Send me the checks, and I will issue you stock in the company. Alside will pay you dividends every three months, different amounts each time. Take the dividend checks to the bank and deposit it in your checking account or savings, and if you need to spend extra money, use that money. I will deduct the amount of the dividend check from the payment you get from each sale. Now you and I have established a relationship. I buy clothes from your store. If you think there is a need to meet me in person, I will arrange a buying trip. Your man Lewis should have his sample by the time you get back to DC. Remember this phone number." He gave me a piece of paper. "It is a secure line you can talk freely to me on. Never call this line from your home or workplace and burn the number as soon as you have it memorized!" The bell sounded and, and the "Fasten your seat belt" sign and the announcement that we would be landing in fifteen minutes came on. Doc said, "The plane is going to make a turn around and return you to DC. Just meditate on everything we've talked about. The game starts now." Doc got up and took the paper he had given me and put it in his pocket, and with the same big smile he always wore, he shook my hand and said, "Welcome to the real world, kid," and disappeared behind the wooden door. I remember Bass always talking about the big times whenever he wanted to identify something at its best. I think I just entered the big times when it came to dealing drugs. (Katy said, "The word around Detroit was, Doc was into a little bit of everything. I hate you got mixed up with him. I feel responsible."

I said, "None of this is your fault. Believe me. I was young, but I knew what I was doing." The plane landed and taxied to a stop. Nobody, as Doc called him, got up looked at me and nodded his head and started for the exit. I was expecting Doc to come through the door and exit the plane, but he never did. When I looked out of the window, I could see the tail end of a limo. I could only see shadows, but I was sure I saw at least four or five. I am not sure if they got off the plane or if they were waiting on the ground. If I had to guess, I would say they were on the plane. But *why*, I was beginning to think, *instead of me recruiting Doc, I had been recruited, and all this was put in motion before I became part of the plan. Maybe I was the last piece of the puzzle, but how could that be?*

The flight headed back to DC. The flight attendant began to set the table. I was not expecting dinner, but she offered me chicken with au gratin potatoes and asparagus or steak and Lobster and au gratin potatoes and asparagus. I chose the steak and lobster. She asked, "And what will you have to drink?"

"Coke with ice," I said. The food was served on a white table cloth and silverware, and it was as good as any I had eaten in DC, and the service was great. I noticed the flight attendant eating alone in the galley and invited her to join me. She accepted and sat down. We introduced ourselves, and she commented that I must be an important person. "I would like to think I am," I said. During our conversation, I noticed my communication had changed. Before tonight, I would speak without giving the words I spoke a second thought. After my conversation with Doc, I was careful and thought about every word as if it was a matter of life or death.

The plane landed in DC at 6:45 p.m. When I exited the airport, my car was waiting for me in the valet parking area. I thought, *This is strange. I never gave the valet my stub! How did they know the time I would return?* I drove back to my apartment trying to wrap my head around everything that happened to me in one day. I had forgotten about my problems with Simone. When I arrived at my apartment, it seemed as if I had been gone for days instead of hours. When I opened the door, I was surprised to find

Simone there with Brenda. This was not what I was expecting. I needed time before Simone confronted me. "Simone, what is going on?" I asked.

She said, "I was worried about you! I have been trying to reach you all day. Brenda said she talked to you, and you were supposed to call, and when I didn't hear from you, I got worried. First, I thought you were with your friend Barbara from New York. But I listened to your messages. She has been trying to get in touch with you too. She called twice. So I knew you were not with her, so where have you been?" I was thinking at that moment if I could tell her the truth, she wouldn't believe it. I had not had anyone question where I had been since my days with my mother. This was shocking.

"I had some things to take care of. I needed to clear my head. I needed to be alone."

"So what is with this Barbara chic?" Brenda asked, not Simone. I think Brenda was jealous. She had been trying to get me to cheat on Simone with her for months, and nothing had happened. Simone asked Brenda to be quiet, and Simone and I went into my bedroom to talk. I was sure Brenda had her ear to the door. Simone started telling me how hurt she was when she heard the voicemail from Barbara. I told Simone she was a hypocrite.

"I felt hurt when I saw you with Ron, but you want me to understand that your relationship with him is okay because he is your sugar daddy."

"That's not the same thing," she responded.

I said, "You want me to accept him in your life because he pays your bills. That's disrespecting me by asking me to accept him. I accepted him in your life because I was not in position to pay your bills, but do not think for a minute it was okay with me.

"But I love you!" she said.

"And I love you, but you cannot have it both ways, Simone." She started to cry, and I felt sad. In my heart I knew things would never be the same with us. She opened her purse, took my key off her ring, put it on the bed, kissed me on the lips, and walked out. I sat on the bed. I heard the door close, and she was gone. I had so much on my mind. I was too young to have to handle all this pressure. Since I moved to Washington, I tried to act older than my age, but inside I knew I was fooling myself. I laid back on the bed hoping to relax. What a day! I could hear the phone ringing as I rested, and I let it ring. I needed some time to myself. I always rested better after a hot shower, but I was too weak and emotionally drained to move from the spot I was in.

The next morning, I checked the answering machine. Simone said she called to check on me a number of times, but I had no messages. She must have erased them. I couldn't wait to get to work. I need to experience some normalcy in my life as I knew it. When I walked into the store, it was like the first breath of fresh air I had breathed in days. Mr. Natham very seldom got to the store before me, but there he was today, reading the paper as he always did before our Monday morning meeting.

"Hi, John. How was your weekend? I started to call you to play a round of golf, but my day got busy, and before I knew it, I was doing a million other things."

"My weekend was full of drama," I said. "Simone and I called it quits."

He looked at me and smiled, "What happened? Did she catch you cheating?"

"No, but she thought I was."

"Maybe it is for the best," he said as he folded his paper. We headed upstairs for the morning meeting. Did he know something I didn't? "We need to make sure we maximize our holiday season," Mr Natham said. "Christmas was only two months away. We need to go over our fall orders and reorders to make sure we are fully stocked. You were not here last year. We ran out of too many top sellers before Christmas and lost a ton of money. We need to be on top of it this year. I have a feeling this will be our best Christmas ever. In your meeting this morning with everyone, get as much feedback as you can about what they think we can do to make that happen."

"That's a good idea. Where is Zoie this morning?"

"She will be in later. She had to take her friend to the airport." I knew he was talking about Barbara, and I was sure now Zoie told Mr. Natham about Barbara and me. I won't be able to have breakfast with you this morning. I have a meeting with Mr. Kleppy at the SBA. They are trying to recruit me to mentor new businessmen and women who are applying for SBA loans. Depending on the compensation, I may consider it. One thing for sure, work had indeed taken my mind of the weekend I just had. After the morning meeting with the salespeople, I went out for breakfast. As Mr. Natham and I always did, I walked past the other stores to see what they had in their windows that was exciting. On the way back to the store, I noticed an elderly man with a cane walking toward me like he didn't see me in his path. He bumped into me, and Lewis's voice came out of the old man. I need to meet with you as soon as possible. Contact me after work at this number. I felt his hand go into my pocket. He brushed my clothes off as he apologized for bumping in to me. It was something out of a James Bond movie. I would have never recognized Lewis if he had not spoken to me and looked into my eyes. It shook me into reality that I had another life, and it was dangerous. I have to admit it was exciting and scary. This is not a game. When I got back to the store, Brenda was the first to greet me. Now she was siding with me, calling Simone a slut, and told me she didn't know Simone was seeing Ron. I told Brenda I didn't want to talk about it. I didn't have time. I knew Brenda would do whatever it took to get what she wanted, even if it meant throwing Simone under the bus.

I had a number of messages from all my friends I had not spoken to over the weekend and decided to call them. They all wanted to know why they couldn't reach me over the weekend.

I took a weekend trip with a new friend I told them. When I thought about it, it was not a lie. I noticed Mrs. Natham was in her office. I was not sure how she felt about my not seeing Barbara. I stuck my head in her office and said good morning. She looked at me and smiled as always and said hello. She never asked me about my weekend or lack of spending time with Barbara—very professional, not mixing business with pleasure. I wanted to ask her how Barbara felt. Was she angry or understanding when I didn't return her calls? Would she give me the benefit of the doubt? The light lit up on my phone. It was Barbara calling from the airport. I was thinking Mrs. Natham had called her to let her know I was in the office. I was not sure what to say. I had not given it much thought. It didn't take long before I knew I had nothing to worry about. She was more concerned about my well-being than our time together. After the questions of concern, she said she was looking forward to the next time we would see each other. I was caught off guard by the mature reaction from Barbara. I apologized to her for not calling, and she stopped me in mid-sentence. "You don't owe me an explanation, love. See you soon," she said and hung up the phone.

With all the things going on in my life, I needed a relationship with no pressure. During my lunch break, I withdrew a check for twenty five hundred dollars. My banker came over as I waited on the check and asked me if I wanted a loan instead of withdrawing my own money. I declined. When I got back to the store, I addressed the envelope and put it in the company mail. All day, I thought about my contact with Lewis. I knew I had a lot to discuss with him. I was not sure if he would go along with the system Doc had put in place. It was a take-it-or-leave-it deal. I knew Lewis trusted me because I was holding his money, three and a half million dollars, for more than six weeks, and he only asked me about it once. So after work, I got in my car, found a pay phone, and called Lewis. He picked up the phone, and before saying hello, he said, "Let's play golf in thirty minutes." I was twenty minutes from the golf course. On a week day, it could take longer. Evening traffic is no fun in DC. Before I could get to the course parking lot, I spotted Lewis sitting on a bench eating a hot dog and drinking out of a cup. I parked, walked over, and sat next to him. He gave me a bag that contained the same thing he was eating. Without looking at me, he said, "I got the sample. There are only two people that I know can supply that quality of product. One is in jail, arrested two months ago and probably will never get out. And the other is the CIA. I am not claiming to know everything, but if these are CIA drugs, I pass. It's deadly. If you get involved with those people, they use you up and spit you out dead, never alive. So tell me, I have been trying to figure this thing out all day. There is no way you can be CIA, but you can never tell in Washington, DC. So I am asking you, not that you would tell me the truth if you were. Are you CIA?"

"No, I am not CIA, and neither is my contact."

With those piercing eyes, Lewis looked into my eyes and said, "Johnny boy, (he never called me that before) you need to be sure!" In the dos-and-don'ts list Doc had given me, none of it included negotiation. What I knew to be true was, I had known Lewis about as long as I had known Doc. I could not vouch for either one of them concerning their character. So, I gave him the only answer I knew to be true.

"I am as sure about my contact as I am about who you are," I said. "Do you want to move forward? If you do, the rules are a little different."

"Hell, yes I want to move forward! I expressed my concerns, and you have assured me that I have nothing to worry about, so let's move forward."

"Okay. These are the conditions when you are ready to make the first purchase."

"The first purchase?" he said. "I am ready now!"

"Let me explain how this works before you agree. As I said, this transaction maybe a little different than what you are used to. A key will be delivered to you with the name of a hotel or motel. The location will always be different. Leave the money in the room, and lock the door. Come back in twenty four hours, and pick up the package. It will be there. It will always match the amount of money you leave. The price is twenty five thousand a key."

Lewis spoke up and said, "If the drugs are not there, are you responsible for my money?"

"Yes. The room will be rented for one week. There will never be more than a week's delay. So if there is a problem, give it a few days before you contact me. Less contacts, the better."

"So you say I will receive a room key after I tell you I am ready."

"Yes. Within twenty four hours."

"So I guess the key will be delivered to me like the sample. I came out my apartment, and my car had a fucking flat tire. When I removed the spare, the sample was there. What if someone else would have changed the tire? Then the sample would not be there where I told him. Shit! So you guys are that smooth?"

"We don't take any chances." I was beginning to talk like "the man" when I had no idea what was going on. If he had asked me how he received the sample, I would have had no idea.

"You have three and a half million in cash right?"

"I still have it just the way you gave it to me."

"Then I will take a hundred and twenty five keys." I repeated what he had said—a hundred and twenty five keys.

"Yep. Can you handle the weight?"

"No problem," I said.

"I was flying all over the country trying to find this connection," he said. "And it has been right under my nose all the time. The only thing we have to do now is get the money back to you, in order for the buy to go as we discussed. Within twenty four hours, you get your first room key, and we are off and running."

"Man, this sounds too good to be true. My mama always told me if it is too good to be true, it probably is or something like that," he said. "I have one problem, and it is not your problem. My man Fred is still in jail. With him in jail, I am going to have to kill some fools to let them know I am still in control. Fred kept those fools in line; he put fear in their hearts. Johnny boy, I am glad I held on. I figured if those guys could bring the shit from Vietnam or wherever, someone else was doing it too. I never guessed in a million years it would be you." He got up with a big smile on his face and walked away shaking his head and mumbling, "You never know. You never know."

It had gotten dark. Lewis and I had been talking for hours, and it seemed like thirty minutes. I sat there reflecting on everything we had discussed. The CIA kept popping up in my head. *How can the CIA sell drugs?* I thought. That had to be a test to see if I could trust my source. I think he was putting me on alert not to trust anyone. I tried to remember every word I had spoken, because Doc said my life depended on it. Then my mind went dollar signs. If all goes well, I will have two hundred and fifty thousand dollars. That's a lot of money, and it was all mine. ("That's Satan's money!" Katy said. I smiled and kept talking.) I got up and went to my car thinking about the next step in the process. Lewis and I agreed to return his money back to him the same way I received it. He would have someone pick it up at my apartment. I was to leave it at the front desk for pickup. He asked me to take the jewelry out and send only the money. I didn't ask why. I was just glad I was returning that headache.

Whenever I got closer to all of this actually happening, I would reflect on my family and how I was raised and how this would kill my mother and you Katy, if I got caught. I was young, and my whole life would be ruined, but at this point, I had gone too far to turn around now. I got into my car and drove slowly back to my apartment. Now I know why Doc said I needed an apartment that no one knew about but me. If I had it, I surely would go there tonight. I got home around eight o'clock and checked my answering machine. I was hoping Simone would have called, but only messages from a couple of my friends wanting me to meet them for happy hour and saying how hard it was for them to get in touch with me lately. I got dressed and met my friends at the club, but deep down in my heart, I really wanted to see Simone. Hanging out with these guys is always fun for me, and we always had a good time, and tonight was no exception. After telling a few lies about where I was this weekend and trying to explain what happened between me and Simone, everything seemed to fall right back in place. Now the show was over, it was time to go home to the double life I was living. It was now my reality. It was late around 1:00 a.m., and I went up to the storage and got Lewis's money and got it ready for pickup the next day. I took three hundred thousand dollars, and the jewelry out as he had requested. I put the case back in the box, taped it up, and put the name on it he had asked me to: Donna.

I put the jewelry and the balance of the money in a brief case and put it back in storage. I looked at the three hundred thousand dollars, thinking this was close to the amount I would have in just few days if all goes as planned. I laid on my bed thinking about how lonely it was without Simone—and not being able to tell anyone what was happening in my life. I woke up the next morning with my clothes on and jumped up to get ready for work and then realized it was my day off. Normally, Simone and I would try to coordinate my days off with her classes, so we could spend time together. We stayed in the bed most of the day, only leaving to get something to eat. Reflecting on what had happed in each of our lives during the week. I really missed Simone. I took the day to look for an apartment as Doc suggested, and I knew just the place I wanted to look. I had always admired this apartment building that was located just before you crossed the bridge coming into Washington from I-95. You could see it from a distance with the lights on it standing tall as it reached into the sky. It looked close from the bridge, but it was miles away. I never thought about living there before because I knew it was more than I could afford. It was located in Arlington, Virginia, just a few miles from the Pentagon on Army Navy Drive. I showered and got dressed and put on a suit and tie to make a good impression, and then I grabbed my checkbook and the box for Lewis to leave at the front desk. I left the package with Steve at the front desk. He and I had a good relationship, and he always kept me informed about what was going on in the building. I knew he was nosey, but I was not concerned enough not to leave the package. There was no reason for him to be suspicious. I took the elevator to the garage to get my car and saw Mr. Green who always had an encouraging word.

This time, he said, "You are going places, Youngblood. You got what it takes!" I knew he meant well, but those words now, I felt I was letting him down also. As I drove out of the garage, I saw the UPS man loading what looked like the box I left at the front desk for pickup. I tried to tell myself that it couldn't be. I jumped out of the car and ran to the truck before he could get the key in the ignition and asked if I could see the box. Sure enough it was the box. I explained to the driver what happened. He looked at the box. Sure enough, it had no return address, so he took it back inside. I got back in my car and began to imagine what would have happened if the box would have been left in that truck with no return address. How could Steve have made that mistake? I drove to Arlington, not sure if I could get the apartment, not because I couldn't afford it but I wasn't sure if they would accept me as a tenant. I was told that blacks were not treated the same in Virginia as in DC. They really didn't want us there. When I drove down 1300 Army Navy Drive toward the building I hoped would be my new apartment. I passed the Pentagon and could see I-95 in the distance. Pulling in front of the building with the beautiful fountain with stone carved dolphins jumping out of the water with a stone inlaid driveway, I thought, *This is head and shoulders above my place.* I parked in front and walked into the lobby with marble floors, beautiful large plants, and pictures as large as rooms hanging on the wall. I looked around and asked myself, "What are you doing here?"

I heard a woman's voice asking, "May I help you?"

"Yes. I would like to speak to someone about renting an apartment."

She asked me to have a seat and said, "Someone would be with you shortly." Looking around, there were at least six large sitting areas in the huge lobby. I chose the one closest to the door. After about ten minutes, the elevator door opened, and a beautiful woman came out and spoke to the lady behind the desk, then headed toward me. I had seen this lady before. She was the flight attendant that worked Doc's flight. What a coincidence, or was it? She recognized me right away and gave me a big hug.

"What are you doing here?" she asked.

"I am looking for an apartment. I didn't know you worked here."

"My father is the manager here at 1300 Army Navy."

"I don't remember your name," I said.

"I remember yours. It's Johnny, and mine is Shannon. Let's go upstairs to the office and get you an application." I looked over at the woman behind the desk, and she had this bewildered look on her face. We took the elevator to the second floor, on the way up Shannon told me about the building. Mostly military officers that worked at the Pentagon lived in the building. They were given month to month leases, but for civilians, a one year lease was a requirement. After the first year you can renew or continue month to month. The building had sixteen floors with one to four bedrooms ranging from $600 to $2,000 a month. Parking is $50 for each car. Parking is underground and heated. Located on the first floor is a grocery store, drug store, a cleaners, and a restaurant. There is valet service from 6:00 a.m. to 8:00 p.m. We entered the office, and it was as beautiful as the lobby and almost as large. Shannon gave me an application and excused herself and went into another office. It took me about ten minutes to complete the application. Just as I finished, Shannon came out of the office with a very distinguished and very well-dressed elderly man with her. "Johnny, this is my father, Armen Sheffield."

"How do you do, Mr. Johnny? My daughter has told me you were looking for and apartment?"

"Yes, sir. I have admired this building from afar, and it is more beautiful than I imagined. Well, we will be glad to have you as one of our tenants. My daughter will show you the apartments that are available. We have a corner unit on the eighth floor that just came available. They are our most sought after units. It is a two-bedroom. Take a look at it, and see how you like it. He took the application from my hand, turned and walked back into his office, and closed the door.

"Follow me," Shannon said. "I will show you the unit my father is talking about." We reached the corner unit, and Shannon showed me an elevator that serviced the corner unit that allowed those tenants only to operate with their key. She opened the apartment, and it almost took my breath away. The unit had beautiful furniture already in place. "Does it come furnished?"

"No, some of the officers who rent these apartments have to leave on short notice. They leave the furniture for the other family to use or not. If you don't like it, we can have it removed. You should see all the wonderful furniture we have in storage. It is from all over the world. You can furnish your apartment from our storage. I will show you the furniture we have. The apartment was large, elegant and had a wrap around balcony that started from the front living room facing I-95 and ended at the back two bedrooms facing a private park.

"What does this unit rent for, Shannon?"

"One thousand and two hundred dollars a month. It is paid for through the end of the year, so you have two and half months free."

I kept thinking as Shannon was talking. This does not happen in the real world I live in. These people are living by a different set of rules.

"Do you like it?"

"What's not like? I'll take it."

"Let's go back to the office and sign the lease. I am a very good decorator," she said. If you like, I can have maintenance move some furniture from storage to decorate your apartment. Do you have any furniture?"

"I was thinking of buying some new furniture for my new place. But I haven't bought any yet."

"I'll put some things in for you until you get your own, if you like."

"Yes."

When we got back to her office within thirty minutes, the lease was signed, and I had the keys and was in my car trying to wrap my head once again around what had just happened. I remember Bass telling me I was the luckiest man he knew. I was beginning to think so too.

The Death of Simone

I stopped at a pay phone before I left Arlington to give Doc a call to let him know everything was a go with Lewis. "Fasten your seat belt," he said. "We're off and running." I drove back across the bridge to DC. I decided to stop by the store on my day off as I always did to see what was going on. Mr. Natham was in a good mood. The store was busy, and all the salespeople had customers. I stayed for a while. Mr. Natham and I talked about the buying trip to New York that he and I were going to take. It was in one week, and he estimated we would be gone for two days, possibly three. He said, "We need to make sure we are ready for Christmas."

I told him I was looking forward to the trip and headed home. When I walked through the lobby, Steve informed me the package was picked up by the right person this time, smiling. I walked into my apartment and looked around. I never thought about it as being small, but after coming from 1300 Army Navy Drive, the difference was night and day. I took a quick shower, jumped in the bed, turned on the TV, and quickly fell asleep. Hours later, the phone rang, and I let the answering machine pick it up. It was Brenda from work. She kept calling my name and telling me to pick up the phone.

"Pick up," she said. I was not sure I wanted to talk to Brenda.

Then I heard Mr. Natham's voice on the line, saying the same thing, "Johnny, are you there? Pick up." I quickly ran to the front room and picked up the phone.

"Mr. Natham, I was asleep. Is there something wrong?"

He answered, "Johnny, it was just on the evening news that two people were found dead in a house on the west side."

What does this have to do with me? I thought.

"They identified them as Simone and a guy named Ron. It was an apparent robbery. They had been dead for a few days. The mailman smelled the foul odor coming from the house and called the police." I dropped the phone and tried to sit down on the couch and fell on the floor.

I could hear Mr. Natham say, "I am going to his apartment," and Brenda kept calling my name. I was in shock! When I told Bass why Simone and I broke up, he told me Ron was a numbers banker on the west side and carried a big book.

I kept saying, "God, no! God, no!" and as I called God's name, I thought, *I cannot remember the last time I called his name.*" I was a person that prayed every night and every day, but since I started this journey, I was too ashamed to pray. I felt, of all the people I had disappointed, it was God I had disappointed the most. God knew what I was doing. I felt now God did not hear my prayers or the question that was racing through my mind for the answer why. I sat quietly on the floor feeling as though I was half sleep and half awake—until there was a knock on the door. I heard Mr. Natham's voice asking me to open the door. I crawled to the door, struggled to my feet, and opened the door. Mr. Natham put me in a bear hug, and I cried like a baby. He closed the door and walked me to the couch and sat me down. Then he picked up the phone and hung it up. Then it began to ring, one call after another, and I could hear Mr. Natham saying time after time, "He's alright. Yes, he knows." Mr. Natham walked over to the kitchen and fixed both of us a drink. "Here, drink this," he said. He began to tell me, "Everything will be alright."

("Johnny I am so sorry!" Katy said. "That had to be devastating.") It was the most painful thing I ever felt. I told Mr. Natham I never had someone so close to me die before and, in this case, murdered! You think about the fact you will never see this person again. Then Mr. Natham told me about the death of his mother and how hard it is in the beginning, but as time passes, it gets a little easier to bear. You have moments, but overall, things get better, and the pain gets easier as time goes by. He looked at his watch, and I knew he needed to get back to the store. We had been talking for about an hour. I assured him I would be okay and was feeling much better. I thanked him for coming. He patted me on the cheek and said, "Take a few days off. It's okay." I didn't respond because at that point, I was not sure what I needed. I thanked him again and closed the door. I went into the bedroom and laid on the bed with my hands behind my head. I could still smell her cologne as I thought of her. The phone continued to ring, and I let the answering machine pick up as I dozed off to sleep. The next morning, I thought I had a bad dream, and then reality quickly set in. Simone was dead. I went to work. I needed to be around people and not alone at home. When I was exiting the building, the door man called me just before the door closed, and he gave me five messages from friends who came during the evening expressing how sorry they were and asking me to call as soon as possible. One message had a card attached and was from DC Homicide Detective Harry Trimbal asking me to call as soon as possible. I got to the store about an hour later than usual, and everyone was there. Brenda was the first to hug me and tell me how sorry she was and how Simone's death had her reevaluating her life. I knew she was still seeing Lewis, but I was not concerned. Lewis would never trust her enough to tell her anything about our business. I was sure of that. All the sales staff expressed their sympathies and good wishes. Mrs. Natham gave me a kiss on the cheek and didn't say a word. When I got to my office, I called Bass to discuss the card I received from the detective. I needed his advice. Bass was sure that he wanted to ask me questions about my relationship with Simone. Bass asked me to change what happened between Simone and I. He said to make it sound like she had caught me cheating, instead of my calling her affair into question. Bass thought if I told them the truth, they would consider me a suspect. When I hung up the phone, I asked Mr. Natham what he thought I should do. He told me "to just tell the truth." Before we could finish our conversation, the phone rang.

It was Sherry at the front desk, "There are two detectives that want to speak to you."

"I will be right down," I said. Mr. Natham looked out of his window and knew one of the detectives and told Sherry to show them to his office.

"Harry T.," said Mr. Natham as he greeted Detective Trimbal. "How are things back home?"

He smiled as he responded, "Not very much has changed."

Mr. Natham looked at me and said, "Harry and I went to school together back in Raleigh." Harry was a short guy built like a Mack truck. They talked about his days as a football player and how he was a star running back. While they talked, I tried not to pay attention, but all I could see was how official they looked and had handcuffs on their sides and could see their gun under their jackets. Harry introduced his partner and wasted no time getting to the point.

He called me Mr. Brown and said, "I want to ask you about Simone Tate." At that moment, I realized I had dated Simone for four months and did not know her last name. "What was your relationship with her?"

"We dated up until a few weeks ago."

"What happened?"

"She was seeing someone else and wanted me to accept it because the guy was paying her bills. She thought I was seeing someone, and she was jealous. I called her a hypocrite, and she said good-bye, gave me my keys to my apartment, and left. I have not spoken to or heard from her since."

"How long ago was that?"

"Five days ago."

"This guy she was dating, did you know him?"

"No, I knew his name, Ron Styles."

"How did you know his name?"

"Simone told me."

"Did you ever meet him?"

"No."

Mr. Natham interrupted and asked if I was a suspect.

"No, his story checks out with what we were told. If we have any more questions, we know where to find you."

Harry said to Mr. Natham T., I'll see you later," and shook his hand.

He looked at me and just said, "Mr. Brown," nodded his head, and walked toward the door.

"Detective Harry, how did she die?" I asked.

"They were both shot." He didn't give anymore details and walked out the door. Later in the day, we found out more and more details about the robbery. The word on the street was that Simone was shot in bed, and Ron was found in another part of the house. Both were shot multiple times. It is amazing how much information you can get from the streets, more than you get on evening news channel. That evening Brenda called me at home to tell me about the memorial service they were having at the university. She was planning to go and asked me if I wanted to attend. I wanted to pay my respects to Simone, and this is probably the only chance I would get. Brenda said her parents were taking her body back to Alabama for burial.

The next morning, I got dressed for the memorial at 11:00 a.m. I put on an outfit Simone had complimented me on many times and said how great it looked on me. It was a tan crushed velvet double breasted suit. I wore it with a deeper tan turtle neck, with dark brown and tan shoes that looked like spats. When I got there, the auditorium was filled with students and faculty. I looked around and saw Brenda waving at me at the front entrance with some of my friends, Sherman, Cherokee, Bass, Lin, and Lewis. Simone's friends Terri and Trisha were with them also. I was not expecting to see Lewis. We had not spoken since our talk in the park. Trying to remember, I am sure he had only met Simone once when we were invited to his home for Sunday dinner. I spoke to everyone and was happy for their support. Brenda found seats for all of us in the auditorium. I'm not sure, but I think she had someone save the seats just for us. There was a young lady and a choir singing on stage. I thought the song was sad, "There Will Be Peace, Joyful Peace after the Storm." There were two women and one man sitting on one side of the stage and two men and one woman sitting on the other side. They looked like students and teachers from the university, but I was not sure. When the song was over, one of the men, an older man, got up to speak about Simone. He spoke about what a bright student she was, with unlimited promise and potential that had been taken away from us much too soon. He talked about how the company we keep can have a profound impact on your life, even death. He also talked about how Simone's life should be a wake up call for all students to reevaluate their lives and make better choices. I was upset. I felt he was judging Simone. She was no longer able to defend herself. When he sat down, no one clapped. The other professors talked about how well she performed as a student and how she was always ready to assist other students at Howard—promoting the university every chance she got. They both received a round of applause. Then one young man got up and began to speak about Simone as if they were long time friends, I mean as girlfriend and boyfriend. He spoke about when he first met Simone and the trips they took to out of town games, how much she was looking forward to graduating. As he spoke, I could feel the eyes of all my friends looking at me, waiting to see how I would display my emotions. When he finished, I clapped louder than everyone. I wanted to show that my feeling did not matter, it was all about Simone. But deep down inside, I felt betrayed by her again. After the service, Brenda wanted to take me down to meet Simone's parents, but I refused. I didn't want this relationship to go any further. I needed it to end. Everyone wanted to go to lunch before we went our separate ways. I knew they wanted to talk about Simone. I refused. I didn't want to talk about Simone anymore. Lewis came up and put his arms around me and said, "Believe me I know how you are feeling right now. You will feel better in a few days. By the way, everything went according to plan." I knew he was talking about the shipment. I said good-bye and went back to my apartment. I wanted to change clothes before going to work.

Steve was at the front desk. He handed me a package that had been delivered to me. From UPS. It was shaped like a shoe box, marked with a Stacey Adams Label, Fine Men's Shoes. I started to give the box back to Steve. But I saw it was clearly marked with my name and address. No one had a greater selection of shoes than Mr. Men's. If someone wanted to buy me shoes, I would have preferred shoes from Mr. Men's. When I opened the door to my apartment, I could hear Shannon on the answering machine telling me my apartment was ready. Before I could pick up the phone, she hung up. I quickly rewound the answering machine so I could hear the entire message.

"Hi, Johnny. Your apartment is ready," she said. "As we discussed, I used some furniture from storage to furnish your apartment. I hope you like it. I will be out of town, flying for the next few days. I hope to see you when I return." So much had happened! I had forgotten about my new apartment. I needed something to look forward to, and seeing my new apartment was exciting to think about. I sat the shoe box on the bed.

As I was taking my clothes off, I was thinking, *Who would send me shoes?* Trying to think of all the people who would send me shoes, I came up with no one. I took the wrapping paper off that revealed a second wrapping of brown paper with no marking. I slowly opened the box, and to my surprise, it was filled with money—one hundred dollar bills in thousand dollar wrappers— and a note from Doc that read, twenty thousand dollars stock investment. This was my first payment. Lewis had ordered 125 keys, and my take was two hundred and fifty thousand dollars less twenty thousand invested in All Side. That would cover my dividend money, so I would have legal money to spend. I sat on the bed with all this money that was all mine, and it made me feel powerful and weak at the same time. I could not spend it or let anyone know I had it. I decided to take the money, two hundred and thirty thousand dollars to my new apartment after work, "my new place of refuge." I was so excited to see my new place and see what it looked like after Shannon decorated it. If it was anything like she dressed, it had to be classy! When I got to work, I was surprised to see Brenda. I said, "I thought you guys went out to eat?"

She answered, "No, we all went our separate ways. I stayed and talked to Simone's parents and found out that they didn't have any insurance on her. They are raising money at the school to help ship her body home and pay for the funeral. That will cost five thousand dollars. The school said they would help but did not promise any specific amount." At that moment, I knew I would pay the expenses, but I couldn't tell Brenda. I had to take care of it myself. After work, I went home and looked over the program from Simone's memorial service. I needed to know her parent's names! That, I easily found on the program. Now I just needed to know where they were staying while here in DC, and I had to know tonight! I called the school and inquired where they were. They had no information or refused to give it. My only choice was to call Brenda. I needed a good story. I told Brenda that I spoke to some of my friends about Simone's parents not having enough money to ship her home and pay for the funeral.

We decided to chip in and help, but I needed to know where they were staying so I could take the money we collected to them.

Brenda quickly responded, "They are staying at the Ed Murphy Hotel across from the university."

"Thanks," I said, quickly hanging up the phone. I didn't want Brenda asking any questions. I took eight thousand dollars of the money I received from Doc and put it in an envelope. I know Doc told me not to spend the money this way; but I knew I was doing the right thing. I went to the hotel, after receiving the room information from the front desk. I took the elevator to the third floor. When I arrived at Mr. and Mrs. Tate's room, I heard loud conversations, different people talking at the same time. I could tell the room was full of people. I knocked on the door twice before Simone's father answered the door. I recognized him from the memorial service.

"Yes, can I help you?" he asked.

"Yes, sir. My name is Johnny Brown. I am a friend of Simone's."

"Yes, come in. Simone talked about you every time she spoke with her mother. We were hoping we would get a chance to meet you." Simone's mother stood up and walked over and gave me a hug.

"Johnny, I heard so much about you from Simone. She was sure you were her soul mate." I was amazed she knew my name and that Simone had told her parents about me. Now I knew for certain what I meant to Simone. Only then did I know for sure she really loved me.

"Mr. and Mrs. Tate, I was at the memorial service today and wanted to say hello." There were so many people around, so I decided to wait. Brenda told me about the financial hardship Simone's death has caused, so some of my friends and I got together and pitched in. We hope this will help. I handed the envelope to her father. He took it and started to open it. I stopped him and asked if he would wait until I left before he opened it. We talked for a while; then I hugged her mother and shook her

father's hand, said good-bye, and left. I was halfway down the hall
when I heard the room break into a shout as they praised God,
and the words "Thank you, Jesus" kept coming from their lips.
I heard their door open as I turned the corner and entered the
elevator. Now they could grieve Simone's death without worrying
about the money. It felt so good to be able to give and having it
to give. I knew selling drugs was wrong, but having the money
to help Simone's parents made me feel good. (Katy, looking tired,
smiled and said, "That was a nice thing for you to do." I told
Katy I never got the chance to tell Simone that living together
as she suggested was not a bad idea. Katy closed her eyes, and I
continued to talk. Subconsciously, I was sure she was still listening
and didn't want to stop.)

I went back to my apartment and got the balance of Lewis's
money, and mine, and headed for my new apartment. When I
crossed over the Fourteenth Street Bridge, although it was just
a short distance from DC, I felt like I was taking a vacation.
I used my remote to open the garage door and parked under
the building in my parking space. I'd rented two spaces. I used
the key to the elevator that serviced the wing of corner units
where my apartment was located. I headed for the eighth floor.
When I opened the door to my apartment, I was amazed at what
I saw! The curtains were pulled back. I could see the lights on the
expressway off into the distance. My apartment was beautiful! I
could not have imagined anything as beautiful as this. Shannon
had placed a pool table in the far corner of the room, with an
oriental rug under it. She had also placed another to match in the
center of the room with the largest coffee table I had ever seen.
The glass on the coffee table was held up with ivory tusks. I was
sure they were real. There was a sofa that covered the complete
right side of the room, and every piece of furniture looked as
if it was made to fit where she placed it. I sat on the sofa, and
my eye canvassed the room; Shannon had thought of everything.
There was not a place in the room, or on the walls, that had

not been decorated with beauty and style. It was fit for a king! I couldn't wait to see the rest of the apartment. Looking out of the windows at the lights on the expressway and the DC lights across the bridge was like nothing I had ever seen. It all belonged to me, and I couldn't show it to anybody! I took the briefcase with the money and placed it on the dining table. I slowly walked through the rest of the apartment, taking it all in. There were even towels in the bathroom with my initials on them. Shannon had thought of everything. I came prepared to spend the night but decided not to. There was no TV in the apartment, and there was a game I wanted to watch. I could not wait to put the new twenty-five-inch TV that had just came out in every room.

While I was daydreaming about the things I could do, the doorbell rang. *Who could that be?* I looked out of the peephole, and two officers were standing at my front door. My heart stopped beating, and I could feel all I was doing wrong crashing down over my head. I needed to move the money from the table! I quickly put the briefcase in the kitchen cabinet and walked back and opened the door. One of the officers asked if I was Mr. Brown. I said, "Yes, I am."

"We are the security patrol that works the night shift. We saw a car parked in your parking space and wanted to make sure it was yours. It fits the description we had, but it didn't have a sticker. We wanted to make sure. Sorry to interrupt your evening, but we have to check everything, nothing is taken for granted. You should be getting your stickers in a few days. Put them on as soon as you receive them."

"Thanks," I said and closed the door. And at that moment, I started breathing again. I thought about the consequences of doing something illegal, the fear it creates inside of you when you think your sins have caught up with you. I didn't want to ever feel that way again. I decided at that moment, I would never feel that way again. When fear kills you before death, you die twice. I made the decision to sell drugs. Now I have to live with the consequences without fear. The minute I made that decision, I felt cold inside. I knew something inside me switched over, and I couldn't switch it back.

Dinner in New York

When I got back to my apartment in DC, I had a message from Mr. Natham asking if he could pick me up around 8:00 a.m. for the New York trip. I called him back to confirm, watched the game, and hit the sack. I always looked forward to the buying trips to New York. After all that had happened in the last few weeks, I needed to get away. In the back of my mind, I was hoping to see Barbara, but I couldn't call her. I didn't have her number. Mr. Nathan's plan was to stay two or three days. I was hoping we would at least stay two. Sometime his plans changed. I woke up with the sun beaming through the windows. I thought I had overslept, but it was only six fifteen. I took a shower, got dressed, and packed enough clothes just in case we did. Stay three days in New York. I went over to clear my answering machine when I noticed I had not listened to all of my messages. My sister Selenia had called. Her husband Richard was being transferred to California, and they were leaving in one week. They wanted to see me before they left. Selenia was the only family I had in DC. She was the one who encouraged me to come to Washington. She said it was the most progressive city for blacks in the country. Now that she was leaving, I would be all alone. It wasn't like we saw each other every day, but knowing she was there was comforting.

I didn't have time to call her. It was 7:45 a.m., and I needed to hurry. Just as I opened the elevator door, I saw Mr. Natham's car pull up. My timing was perfect. He was driving the Cadillac.

It was a nice car with plenty of leg room. I threw my bag in the trunk as I greeted Mr. Natham. He asked me how I was feeling. I told him the buying trip was just what I needed. Whenever we would go to New York, I would drive, but this time he stayed behind the wheel. It was not long before he began to lay out the agenda for the trip and asked if I had the inventory list of things we needed to concentrate on. I did. We began to go over the list I had put together after the meeting with the salesmen. They all worked on commission and didn't want the store to run out of the hot inventory. Of course, we didn't want to have a huge amount of inventory left over after Christmas. It was a balancing act of knowing our customers and sales staff. After outlining our buying trip, Mr. Natham began to talk about some of the things that happened to me in the last few weeks. I assured him I was okay and thanked him and his wife for their support. Then he said, "If it makes you feel any better, Brenda and some of her friends were able to raise enough money to pay for Simone's trip home and funeral. She told me the family did not have any insurance and needed help. We gave her two hundred dollars toward the expenses."

I thought, *Once again, Brenda had taken the credit for something she didn't do*. I told Mr. Natham I was happy about that I thanked him again for helping. We arrived in New York around noon and went right to work. We were able to confirm that 80 percent of our reorders would be delivered weeks before Christmas. We worked until five when Mr. Natham suggested we stay overnight to finish our buying early the next morning before heading home. Mr Natham had changed his mind. We would only be staying one night in New York. I wasn't happy. I wanted to spend at least two nights in New York and wanted very much to see Barbara, but I had no way to get in touch with her without letting Mrs. Natham know my intention. I always enjoyed the dinners that Mr. Natham and I had after a long day of shopping. The food was always great. We usually stayed at the Park Lane Hotel, but they were booked, so we stayed at the Marriot downtown. Mr. Natham and I caught a cab back uptown to pick up the car and bring it downtown to the Marriot parking lot. Mr. Natham checked us in and gave me my key. He was on the seventh floor, and I was on the fifth. We agreed to meet in the lobby around seven thirty for dinner. He always made the decision where we ate. I was hoping we would dine at the steak house on Seventh Avenue. I thought they had the best steaks in New York. I was happy also that we had a little time before dinner. Maybe I could get a little rest. I took a quick shower, called the front desk for a wake up call, and laid across the bed for a quick nap. Before I could fall asleep, the phone rang. I thought it was Mr. Natham changing the itinerary for dinner. I cleared my throat to sound alert and answered the phone. To my surprise, it was Barbara. Mrs. Natham had called her to let her know I was in New York and that I might need some cheering up. I was happy she called and very much wanted to see her. I wanted to experience that feeling she gave me the last time we made love. She suggested coming over before I went out for dinner and wait for me to return. I agreed and told her to come on over. Five minutes later, there was a knock at the door.

It was Barbara. She was in the lobby when she called and was sure I would agree to her plan, and she was right. Before she could get in the door, my hands were all over her. I had not been with a woman since Simone and I broke up, and that was four weeks ago. I only had a tee shirt and shorts on. I began to undress her before the door was closed. Soon I discovered she didn't have much on either. Under the beautiful gabardine coat, she had on nothing but bra and panties with high heels. She pushed me on the bed and tore my tee shirt off from top to bottom, and without removing her bra or panties, she put me inside her. Within seconds, we exploded inside each other with sounds of pleasure. (Katy sighed, but did not say anything.) We made love until it was time for me to dress for dinner. I asked Barbara if she wanted me to bring dinner back to her.

"No, just yourself. By the way, there is an overnight bag outside the door. You can bring it in." She came prepared to spend the night, and that was fine with me. I rushed to the lobby to meet Mr. Natham. The sooner we finished dinner, the faster I could get back to Barbara. I would rather be with her than to eat dinner. Mr. Natham was waiting in the lobby, on time as usual. When he recommended the steak house where I really wanted to eat, it was like the best evening ever. I told him it was my favorite and was hoping he chose that one. He said it was his favorite too. He said he only chose Italian when we were with Mrs. Natham. That was her favorite.

We hopped a taxi outside the hotel. Mr. Natham had this boyish smile on his face as if he knew there was something I was not telling him, or maybe I was the reason for the smile on his face. This could only be the case if Mrs. Natham had probably told him about me and Barbara hooking up. Rather than comment, we talked about the inventory we had purchased and what we needed to do the next morning. We arrived at the restaurant within ten minutes. He made reservations for eight, and we were on time. The waiter that always waited on Mr. Natham spotted him and seated us in his section. The ambiance was great. The lights were turned down low, but not so low that you couldn't see the food and the people at your table. It was not easy to see who were seated two tables over. Once we were seated, we placed our orders. Mr. Natham ordered New York strip with all the trimmings, and I ordered a porterhouse with the same. The waiter knew the wine Mr. Natham loved and quickly brought a bottle to the table. We were enjoying the wine and discussing the inventory we had coming for Christmas when Mr. Natham had this surprised look on his face. I looked across the room in the direction he was staring and saw what looked like Doc being seated two tables from us. I took a good look to make sure it was not the wine, and for sure, it was Doc. This was the last person I was expecting to see. Mr. Natham suggested I invite him over.

I got up and went over to his table, and when he saw me, he seemed as surprised as I was. I invited Doc and his guest to join us at our table, and he accepted. I told him we were in New York on a buying trip for the holiday, and Doc said he was in town on business only for a day, and this was his favorite place to eat. The waiter came over and took their orders. Doc ordered two filet mignons, and when asked how he would like them prepared, he said to turn it over and take it off the heat, and the waiter responded, "Blood running." His business partner ordered a porterhouse well done.

Doc commented, "If you cook a steak more than a few minutes, you just ruined a good piece of meat." He then ordered another bottle of the wine that we were drinking. The conversation then turned to our running into each other in New York of all places and the clothes Doc wore—clothes he had purchased from Mr Men's. Doc said he and his associates were the talk of the town in Detroit with the new fashion statement they were making. After a few glasses of wine, Mr. Natham excused himself to the men's room. He was three steps away from the table when Doc turned to me, and the expression on his face was completely different. "Look, my being here is not a coincidence. It is a matter of life or death." At that point, he had my undivided attention as I tried to listen intensely to every word he spoke. "I don't have a lot of time," he said. "So listen carefully! Lewis has a man in Philadelphia named Frank Knobs. There is a plan for him to be killed by his right-hand man tomorrow after a weekly basketball game they play every Saturday morning. After the game, they always go for drinks at the same bar. Frank always leaves first. They plan to kill him outside the bar and make it look like a robbery. Call Lewis and give him this information. He will know exactly what to do. Call him tonight from the lobby phone and not from the phone in your room. It is very important that he hear from you tonight! If he asks you where you got the information from, tell him you heard about it in New York from a friend. Lewis told you Philadelphia was his town, and you assumed Frank was his man. Change the expression on your face! Here comes your boss. Look lively." Mr. Natham sat down as dinner was being served. My brain was in a trance. The information Doc had just given me once again confirmed I was involved in a dangerous business. When I looked down at my plate, I had eaten half of my steak and didn't remember taking one bite, or how it tasted. I was numb. (Katy was tired, and I could see she was falling asleep. I kissed her on the forehead and called it a night. I had planned to stay away the next day because our mother arrived from New Orleans, and I wanted her to spend the day with her, but Katy insisted I come over later that evening and continue. I did. As always, I was surprised. It was as if Katy had written down where I had stopped on paper the day before.)

I tried to maintain the same spirit of joy I had before Mr. Natham had gone to the bathroom, but it was difficult to maintain. We finished dinner, and Doc insisted on picking up the check. He pulled out his American Express and gave it to the waiter, adding a generous tip. Before leaving, Doc reminded us not to forget his spring wardrobe. Mr. Natham assured Doc we would not forget. We took a taxi back to our hotel. Mr. Natham made the comment that Doc was the most charismatic person he had ever met. He is a lot of fun to be around he said. He seems to live an exciting life. I agreed. I was sure I recognized the "associate" Doc was with, and then I remembered, it was the guy on the plane, "Nobody." I was happy Mr. Natham was not in a talkative mood because I was still trying to digest the conversation Doc and I just had. So many questions was going through my brain, I didn't know where to start. My brain was spinning a thousand miles per minute! I was thinking, *Doc must have been waiting outside the hotel and followed us to the restaurant; that's the only explanation. How did he know I was in New York?* For now, all I could do, or think about, was calling Lewis.

When we arrived back at the hotel, we took the elevator up to our rooms, and Mr. Natham talked about our plans the next day. I said good night and got off on my floor. I waited in the hall until the elevator got to Mr. Natham's floor. I then pushed the down button to return to the lobby. I went to the front desk to get enough quarters to make a long distance call. I dialed the only number I had for Lewis when a voice came on the phone instructing me to deposit two dollars and fifty cents. I had only called Lewis two times, and he never picked up the phone the first time. It was always a call back from him that took hours. The answering machine picked up, and I said, "Give me a call at this number. It's important that we talk tonight."

I hung up and took the seat by the phone and waited for Lewis to call. The hotel phones were located in front of the hotel bar entrance. I could see people drinking and having fun, enjoying each others company. I knew at some point everyone at the bar saw me sitting by the phone. I had no choice but to wait on Lewis's call. As I sat there waiting, I remembered Barbara. I had totally forgotten about her being in my room! I sat there with my legs crossed, glancing through a few magazines I picked up from one of the tables. I was trying to make myself look like I was perfectly content waiting for the phone to ring. Although there were six other phones in the area, I had to tell three people that I was waiting on an important call on the one next to me. I sat there forty-five minutes before a gentleman in a grey suit asked if I was a guest in the hotel. He introduced himself as hotel security. After assuring him who I was, he walked away. After waiting for two hours, the phone rang. I answered as if I was sitting on the side of the bed. I was trying not to let on how frustrated I was. Lewis and I never called each other by name as we talked.

"What's up?" he asked.

I said, "I have some information I am not sure it concerns you. I just had dinner with some friends here in New York and learned about a problem in Philadelphia. You once told me Philly was your town. If the name Frank Knobs means anything to you, I've got some information for you. I have learned, after a basketball game he plays on Saturday mornings with his right-hand man and others in his crew, that there is a plan to kill him. After the game, they usually go to a bar for drinks and food, that is when it is going to happen. I understand he always leaves the bar first, and outside is where it will happen. They are going to try to make it look like a robbery, and his right-hand man is the one calling the shots."

Lewis said, "How in the hell do you know this shit?"

I said, "Ears to the ground, my man, ears to the ground." I was trying to sound hip. I had no idea what that really meant. Most of the comments I made during this time in my life were things I had heard other people say.

Then Lewis said, "Give me a call when you get home." He knew I was out of town, Brenda had told him. I knew he had a ton of questions for me when I returned, but for now he needed to save his man Frank. After hanging up the phone, I felt mentally drained. I felt I had aged more than five years in three hours. I opened the door to my room slowly trying not to wake Barbara.

She raised her head and asked, "What time is it?"

"Twelve o'clock. We met some friends from out of town that happened to be having dinner at the same restaurant." I removed my clothes and crawled in the bed behind Barbara and wrapped my arms around her and we both fell asleep. When I woke up, the next morning she was gone, leaving a note that read, "See you soon." I quickly got dressed. Mr. Natham and I had a few more stops to make before returning to DC. Our plan was to leave New York no later than twelve noon and arrive in DC before five. We arrived around four o'clock, a few hours before the store closed. I asked Mr. Natham if I could leave early. I needed to visit my sister Selenia and her husband Richard before they left for California.

He said, "Yes, that is very important! By all means, go!" I went home and took a shower, checked my answering machine, which was full. I decided to respond later. I got dressed as quickly as I could. I wanted to get ahead of the evening traffic. I wanted to give Selenia and Richard some money, about fifty thousand, but I knew I would never be able to explain where the money came from, but I could explain ten or fifteen. I did beat the traffic and was four blocks from my sister's apartment when I saw three sheriffs' cars and a group of people standing around. For some reason and to this day, I don't know why I stopped to see what was going on. It was clear when I walked close to the group of people someone was getting evicted. I saw a lady crying with two children. I asked one woman standing next to me whether she knows the lady.

"I know her well. She is a good mother…works hard everyday, and her husband had not been paying the rent with the money she had given him." I asked where the husband was. "No one has seen him since yesterday." I walked over to the officer who was holding a clipboard and given directions to the other officers and asked how much she owed in back rent. He asked who I was. I just said someone that might be able to help. He told me, they owed $963 and $125 for the eviction action.

I told the office that I would pay the back rent. He looked into my eyes. then, from the top of my head to the bottom of my feet, then said, "Okay, that will be one thousand and eighty-eight dollars in cash." I walked back to my car to count the money. I didn't want him to see how much money I had in my pocket. I came back and put $1,088 in his hand. He counted the money twice, and then ordered the men to stop and put everything back into the apartment. I walked back to my car as quickly as I could. I could see some of the women walking toward the officer. I assume to inquire about what happened. I didn't want to draw any attention to what I had done. Doc told me never to show any hint of extravagance. The officer didn't ask for identification, so no one knew who I was. At eighteen, I was not one who wanted to be noticed or recognized for what I did. I would learn years later that was why Doc chose me for this operation. When I got to my sister's apartment, there were two trucks outside, and men were loading their furniture for the trip to California. Richard was standing outside making sure everything was placed in the trucks without being broken. We greeted each other with a hand shake. I had not seen Richard in months. He was always either out of town or out of the country. But his personality was always the same whenever you saw him, always smiling and very positive about everything. I don't think Richard ever had a bad day. If he did, you would never know it. I got right to the point after we greeted each other and asked Richard to take a walk with me.

I decided to give the money to Richard instead of my sister Selenia. If I gave it to her, she would tell everyone in the family. Then I would have to explain every detail about where the money came from. And I didn't want to go through all of that. I would only have to explain it once to Richard, I knew he could keep a secret, even from my sister.

He said, "Sure," and when we were far enough away from their apartment, I gave Richard the money. He looked at it and asked what it was for. I told him I had saved some money and had money left over from when I hit the number. And I wanted him and my sister to have it to start their new life in California. He tried to give it back, but I insisted he take it. It was fourteen thousand dollars. He thanked me and gave me a big hug and said he would use the money to buy a house. Richard told me he was sure this would be his last deployment. Then I asked Richard not to tell my Selenia about the money and told him why. He promised me he wouldn't while putting the money deep in his pocket. We went back to the apartment and spent the next three hours saying our good-byes. Selenia was greatly concerned about leaving me in Washington without family. I assured her it would be okay. Richard told her about his friends he had recruited to check on me. Two of them I knew became my friends, Carl Hayes and Larry Troy. They walked me to the door, and I kissed Selenia, and Richard walked me to my car. He opened my hand and put a card in it with a phone number and codes.

"We would call them passwords today."

He looked me in the eye and said, "If you ever get in trouble, call this number and say these words, and they will make sure you get help."

All I knew about my brother-in-law was that he was a master sergeant in the Air force and spoke seven different languages fluently. Which I always thought was cool. He never talked about what he did. I thanked him and got in my car and drove away. I was feeling good about what I did to help my sister and the lady at the apartment. I felt powerful knowing I could make a difference in someone's life, but I felt just as bad about how I got so much money. Then my thought and focus quickly returned to Doc and all that was happening. Before when I was uncomfortable with someone or something, I would just not be bothered with them or it anymore, but I was not sure I could walk away if I wanted to from Doc and the position I had put myself in.

Excited to be home after being away for a few days, I was looking forward to a relaxing evening at home in bed and watching TV. I checked my answering machine. I had calls from all my friends—Linwood, Sherman, Cherokee, Steve, and Frank—and a number of hang ups.

Then there was a message from Doc saying, "I hope everything went well. Need to talk give me a call when you get home." I wasn't ready to talk to Doc. I needed a break from all the madness. Little did I know, the madness had not yet began. I decided everything could wait until tomorrow and couldn't wait to take a shower and hit the bed, my own bed. After relaxing on the bed for a few minutes, I decided a night out on the town was just what I needed. I got dressed, called Linwood and Sherman, and there was no answer, but I knew where they would be, so I headed for the Fox Trap. Before I could get out the door, there was a call from the front desk. They had a package for me and wanted to know if I wanted it to be sent up or would I prefer to pick it up. I told them I was on my way down to pick it up. It was my second payment.

"I had just received a payment from Doc two weeks before." With this payment, I had close to a half a million dollars, with thirty five thousand in my checking account. The money from the stock account, Doc said, I could spend any time without any concern. The other money was just money. There was nothing I could do with it. I had to find somewhere to hide it and that was beginning to create a problem. I was not expecting to receive money from Doc so fast. How could someone sell drugs that fast? I was sure Lewis was expanding his operation to more cities taking advantage of the connection he had with the best product around. That's what I would do. I took the package and put it under my bed. I can take it to storage when I got back. Tonight I was going out with my friends and forget about all the drama my life had turned into.

Raven

It took me a few clubs before I found my friends hanging out at Larry Browns. I was glad to see them, and they were happy to see me as well. The questions were coming from all directions. Where have you been? I've been calling you. You don't have time for your boys anymore? I gave them the only answer I could give: busy working getting ready for the Christmas at the store. After some small talk about what every one else was doing, we were back to being boys again. I saw Brenda and her crew dancing on the dance floor. She saw me and waved, and I waved back. I noticed a young lady with Brenda's crew I had not seen before. She was tall brown skinned and had a short haircut, with legs that looked like she had been running track every day of her life. And the miniskirt she had on only accentuated them even more. She was getting lots of attention from all the men in the club. A different guy was asking her to dance on every record. I noticed she was looking at me or someone at our table every chance she got. I was sure it was my eyes that were meeting hers as she stared at our table. I didn't want to ask her to dance. Everybody was doing that. After about five minutes of staring back and forth, I got up from the table, walked over, and reached for her hand, and she gave it to me. Instead of going to the dance floor, I found a bean chair in the corner of the room and sat down. We looked into each others eyes for about a minute before we said a word. I held her right hand, and with her left, she began to rub the top of my hand with her left hand, just like my grandmother used to do before she gave me a serious talking to. She waited for me to start the conversation.

"What is your name?"

"Raven," she said.

"My name is..."

And before I could say my name, she said, "Johnny. I asked one of the girls at the table, and she told me your name. I moved to Washington this summer. I live with my sister Terri. She's the one in the yellow skirt at the table looking over at us."

"Where are you from?" I asked.

"Winston Salem, North Carolina. Where are you from?" she asked.

"I am from Mississippi."

"I don't think I ever met anyone from Mississippi."

"Neither have I." We both thought that was funny.

"Would you like some champagne?" I asked.

"I don't know. I never had it before," she said. I called the waiter and ordered champagne with cranberry juice. I like to mix the two. When the waitress brought the champagne over, she moved us to a VIP table. Raven and I talked and danced for hours. I asked if she would like to go to my apartment. "Yes. Let me tell my sister I am going with you. I'll be right back." Watching as she walked away, I could feel the lustful chemistry we had shared all evening rising up inside me. I could feel an erection growing in my pants. ("Lord, how many women did you have?" Katy said. "And you don't have to tell me all that. "You were just mannish." I smiled and continued with the story.) That had never happened to me before. She was gone for about five minutes, but it seemed longer. I went over to let the guys know I was leaving. I gave Lin enough money to pay their bill. We made plans to get together at my place for the weekend.

"Looking forward to that," I said. When Raven and I walked out of the club together, you would have thought we were longtime lovers. not two people who had just met. I wanted to impress Raven, and as we walked hand in hand out of the club, I thought about taking her to my new place in Arlington, but I didn't, remembering what Doc had said: having a place that no one knew about was important to my survival. We walked to my car, and she was surprised that I had a new car and a 225 at that.

"Is this your car or your father's?" she asked.

"It's mine."

I opened the door for her. When she slid into the seat, her miniskirt slid higher up her thigh, and she didn't pull it down. When I got in. She slid as close to me as she could without interfering with my driving. As we drove to my place, she rubbed the inside of my thigh. I only lived a few blocks from the club, but I was not sure I was going to make it home. When I pulled into the underground parking lot, we started kissing. We were both ready to explore more of each other. We got out of the car and walked toward the elevator. I could see she was impressed with where I lived. I think if I had taken her to my apartment in Arlington that would have been too much. We took the elevator up to the lobby. And when the elevator door opened, I was shocked to see Lewis and a young lady sitting in the corner of the lobby. Before the young lady at the front desk could announce I had a couple waiting for me, Lewis was up and shaking my hand. "I was on this side of town and took a chance you might be home and decided to wait a few minutes. I am glad I waited," he said.

Now I truly knew what Doc meant when he said, "You will need a place no one knows about but you." I introduced Lewis to Raven, and he introduced me to Linda, the lady he was with. I invited them up to my apartment. I knew this meeting needed to happen. I would have liked to control the where and the when, but it was happening now. I opened the door and asked everyone to get comfortable, and if anyone would like something to drink. Raven and Linda were already talking. About what, I didn't know. Raven walked over to the window and commented on the view, and Linda walked over to take a look. That's when I asked if they would excuse Lewis and I for a few minutes. They both said *sure* at the same time.

We walked into the bedroom and closed the door. Lewis started the conversation by saying, "I am not going to sleep until you answer a few questions for me. The shit you come up with, only the FBI would know."

"Are you saying I am FBI?"

"No, I knew you were connected, but how connected. Is it the top?" I was not sure what answer he wanted, so I took control of the conversation.

"You want to know how I knew about your man in Philly. Was my information correct?"

"Yep, saved my man's life! He never saw it coming, but he took care of those fool and set things straight." I assumed he meant they were dead. "My man Frank was so thankful! You saved his life. Shit like this never would have happened if Fred was out of jail. Everybody knew he would make things right if anything happened that wasn't supposed to. Tell me now, how did you know this shit was going down?"

"I was having dinner with some friends in New York, and they started talking about a change of command in Philly. That some fool is about to get his head blown off, and another guy at the table said, 'That's what happens when you put to much trust in the fools around you.' One of the other guys at the table said Frank's full name. I sat there knowing you had people in Philadelphia, and I wanted to make sure it was not connected to your people, and the only way to be sure was to get the information to you as soon as possible. Someone that was part of the plan talked too much, even calling the guy's name, and it's a good thing he did."

"I know. That's right," said Lewis.

I thought, *How can anyone play God, deciding who lives and who dies when we are all drug dealers? Just because one guy is more important to our operation than another, the other dies, and I am at the top of all this.* Lewis asked about his jewelry and the quarter million I still had. I assured him it was as safe as my own money, and he could get it anytime.

"Let's get back to the ladies," he said. When we entered the room, Linda and Raven were acting like old friends. I don't think either of them knew they were in the company of two of the largest drug dealers on the east coast, maybe the country. I walked Lewis and Linda to the door wondering if the explanation I had given him was good enough. It was all I could give him. I could never tell him the truth. I asked Raven what she and Linda talked about. She said that Lewis and Linda had met only a few weeks ago.

I told her, "We just met tonight, and it feel like I've known you all my life."

"How can you explain that?" she said. I took her by the hand and led her to the bedroom. We made love, stopped, and talked, then made love over and over again until the break of dawn. We had a lot in common, Raven was from a small town, and I was from a small town in Mississippi, and we both came to Washington to attend Howard University, but we both got jobs and decided to enroll later after we earned some money. Raven was offered a job with a company that processed college loan applications for the government, and she accepted it. I liked Raven a lot. Her southern charm was refreshing. Plus she was fine and very freaky in bed. We took a shower. I drove Raven home. We made plans to have lunch together. Raven's job was only six blocks from Mr. Men's. When I dropped her off at home, I remembered I had not returned Doc's call, and this is the longest I had gone before calling him back. I rushed home and parked my car and walked to work. It felt like I was walking on air. I was ready for a relationship. I missed what Simone and I had, and I missed her!

When I got to work, I was upbeat and ready to work. Brenda couldn't wait to give me her spin on Raven and her sister. Before

Brenda could say anything, Mr. Natham told me to call Doc because he needed to speak to me.

I told him, "I would have you to call him as soon as you got here."

Mr. Natham was excited about Doc's call. He thought it was related to another big sale for the store. I went to my office and called him. He answered. I said, "Hello, Doc."

"Hey…thanks for calling. It was great running into you guys the other day. It started me thinking about my spring wardrobe again." I could tell he was filtering his conversation. He never gives more information than necessary. "John," he said, "I am going into a meeting. I will call you when I return."

"Okay, Doc." I knew that meant "Call me on a clean phone ASAP." I went back downstairs to join the morning meeting. Mr. Natham asked me about the call from Doc. I told him he couldn't talk; he was rushing to get to a meeting. The store was looking great and well decorated, and Christmas music was playing, and the good part was we had plenty of inventory. Business was great! Christmas was always special to me. It reminded me of the times I had with my family in Mississippi with my sisters and my brother. It was my first Christmas away from home. We pulled names at the meeting to exchange gifts. I understood, it was a tradition at Mr. Men's. I pulled Brenda's name of all people. This was my first Christmas in Washington, and I was looking forward to it. Mr. Natham had a meeting, so I went out for breakfast alone. I walked in a different direction than usual. I had to use the pay phone to call Doc and didn't want anyone to see me. I walked three blocks and went into the Willard Hotel and used the lobby phone. When I spoke to Doc, I could tell he was not happy with the delayed phone call by the tone of his voice.

"Did you get the information to Lewis in time?"

"Yes. He said it saved Frank's life, and I am sure the other guys are not around. Lewis stated that when Fred was around, things like this would never happen."

"Look," Doc said, "we need to talk. I sent you a package. You should receive it today. It's a first-class ticket to LA. I have a meeting I need you to attend. I will give you the details when we meet, so keep your weekend open. If you have any questions, hold them until we meet. It is important you be on time, so follow the instructions in the package, and you should be okay. Look, I have to go. See you on Sunday," he said. I hung up the phone, wondering what this meeting could be about and why of all places, in LA. I had never been to LA or California. Knowing Doc, this was no sightseeing trip. I walked slowly back to the store, knowing at some point during the day Mr. Natham would ask if I talked to Doc. When I got back to the store seeing the Christmas decorations and hearing Nat King Cole's "White Christmas" playing, I quickly forgot about all the things going on in my life.

My focus then turned to my lunch date with Raven, and it was getting close to twelve o'clock. I went upstairs to my office to see the reaction from the men when she walked through the door and to get a full view of her before she sees me. It might seem crazy, but I was an eighteen years old, and that was my mind-set. Looking out of my window, she didn't keep me waiting long. When she threw open the door and walked in, there were two guys behind her, and she was talking over her shoulder as if she was saying, "No, thanks," to their questions. All the salesmen's eyes were on Raven. Even Mr. Brady and I thought he was gay. I saw her ask one of the salesmen if I was in, and before they could page me, I was at the bottom of the staircase. She was even more beautiful than the last time I saw her, and that was just a few hours ago. I put my arm around her and told Jackie the cashier I was going to lunch. Raven had beautiful legs and wore the right clothes to show them off. When we walked out of the store, I could feel all eyes were watching as we walked out the door. I asked Raven what she had a taste for. She quickly replied, "Seafood, and I knew just the place." It was a little pricey, but that was okay. I wanted to impress her and make her happy. When we got there and placed our orders, Raven began to tell me some of her dreams, buying a car, getting an apartment, and saving enough money to go home for Christmas. And after college, she wanted to move back home to Winston Salem. That's why she was working as many hours of overtime her company would allow. I knew I could make all her dreams come true that day, but I had to keep my promise to Doc and not raise any red flags about my finances. Raven was a breath of fresh air. There's nothing pretentious about her; what you saw was all there was of her. She had not been in Washington long enough to be spoiled like most of the beautiful women here. Before the food arrived, Raven commented about my apartment being close by.

I said, "Yes, about three blocks." So we asked the waiter if he could make the order to go. Within minutes, we were walking to my apartment as fast as our legs could carry us. When we got there, we made love like the world was coming to an end. We didn't eat a bite of our lunch. We put the lunch in the refrigerator and made plans to meet after work and eat it for dinner. That was the best lunch I never had. I was falling for Raven, and I had never felt this way about any of the ladies I had dated before, not even Simone. I knew in my heart after one night and a lunch date, this was the lady I was going to marry. But I could not let her know my feelings. Mr. Bass told me to always let the woman express her feelings first. That way, you don't get hurt or lose your position of power over the relationship, if that makes any sense. It did to me at the time. I respected Mr. Bass opinion. When I got back to the store, everyone knew who Raven was. Thanks to Big Mouth Brenda.

Then Brenda walked over to me and said, "I told her sister you were a great catch." This was Brenda's way of taking credit for us being together.

I smiled and thanked her, "You're the best," I said. I tried to walk away, but Brenda wanted to know how I felt about Raven.

"You know she just got here from North Carolina a few weeks ago, and she is going home soon. She's a country girl. Is that what you like?"

"Brenda, you are the last person I would tell my business to, so why are you sweating me? You have a customer waiting." I turned and walked away, smiling and shaking my head at the same time, thinking, *That's Brenda being Brenda.* I could not wait to get home. I was looking forward to my evening with Raven, and I wanted to get home and set the mood. To my surprise, when I got home that evening. Raven was sitting in the lobby. I was happy to see her, but I don't like surprises. She walked over and kissed me, then explained she told her sister not to pick her up, that she was going to meet me at my apartment. "I hope it's okay," I said it was, but in my heart, it wasn't. We walked past the front desk, and the clerk stopped me and gave me a large envelope and a box shaped like a shoe box. It was from Doc. I decided not to open it until I was alone. Hearing from Doc reminded me of what I was doing and what I was, a drug dealer. I tried to manage my emotions as I hugged Raven tight while we walked out of the elevator to my apartment. When I opened the door, Raven was all over me, and within seconds, we were in the bedroom making love with our clothes on. We never got a chance to eat our leftovers. I took her home around 2:00 a.m., and I could tell she was not happy with the decision. She had assumed that we would spend the weekend together. I explained to Raven I had other plans I couldn't change. I could have told her my plans did not include another woman. I know that would have made her feel better. But we had only known each other for two days, and I was not sure I wanted her to think she was the only woman in my life, even though I felt like I was falling in love with her. She gave me a long wet kiss, got out of the car, and walked to her apartment slowly with her head down. I decided to make it up to her later by doing something special.

Cheyenne

I arrived at my apartment around 2:30 a.m. and opened the envelope from Doc. I was very happy to discover the plan had changed. Instead of me flying commercial, Doc would be picking me up at 11:40 a.m. at Washington National. I was happy about the change and very curious as to why I was going to California with Doc. Whatever it was, I could never imagine. I opened the box, and it was filled with hundred dollar bills. I didn't bother to count it. I slid it under my bed. I took a shower and laid across my bed and fell asleep. I woke up with the TV still on. I glanced over at the clock; it was 8:15 a.m. I laid back across the bed with my hands behind my head thinking about my upcoming meeting with Doc. It was what I always did when I was confused about what to do or what action I should take. It was these times when I wished I had someone to talk to I could trust, someone other than Doc. There was a knock at my door. I wondered who could be visiting this early on Sunday morning. I looked through the peephole. It was Mr. Bass. It was Mr. Bass, he was married and had an eight-year-old son, but I don't think he ever went home. He would come to my place anytime morning or night. I opened the door greeted him and hurried into the bathroom to take a shower. I could here him calling my name, mumbling about something as he entered the apartment. When I came out of the bathroom, he had fixed himself a drink. I always enjoyed Mr. Bass's visits. He was funny and always made me laugh. But I really didn't have time for visitors. Mr. Bass could stay in the apartment as long as he wanted to, because I trusted him. But I needed to be at the airport on time. It wasn't long before he began telling me about his early morning meeting he had just concluded with a friend who had backed out on a deal to loan him twenty thousand dollars. He was going to use the money to buy a ten-unit apartment building from this guy he knew, who was trying to sell it off before his divorce was final. Bass couldn't stop telling me what a good deal it was. After his third drink, he fell asleep on the sofa. I got dressed as quickly as I could. I decided to wear the three-piece suit I had just purchased from Mr. Men's. I thought it would be a good time to wear it. It was dark brown with a light blue pinstripe. I threw on a light blue French cuff shirt, an orange tie with light brown polka dots, and brown shoes. I think I looked at myself at least ten times in the mirror before I left the apartment. I left Mr. Bass in the apartment. He had fallen asleep. I wrote him a check for twenty thousand dollars and a note telling him to go forward with the deal. I was his new partner, and we would work out the details when I got back. I informed him I would be out of town with a friend. The money in my checking account now totaled around sixty five thousand dollars. Although I had extra money to spend, I couldn't think of anything to spend it on. At eighteen that was not normal! I arrived at the airport with thirty minutes to spare. The valet attendant met me, took my keys, and gave me a claim ticket, I tipped him ten dollars and walked away feeling like the sharpest man alive. Nobody, as Doc called him, was standing in the airport lobby when I entered the door. He walked over to me and said *follow me* without saying hello. We walked down the stairs and through the hallway lined with portraits of ex-presidents and our president then, Richard Nixon. As we exited and walked toward the plane, I noticed it was twice the size of the plane I took to Detroit. I knew Doc had money and could afford anything he wanted, but this was impressive. This was truly high-rolling, as

Bass called it. We entered the plane, and the flight attendant welcomed me aboard. This time, it was not Shannon. She took my overnight bag and suit jacket and put them in the closet and directed me to my seat. I looked around the plane. It was very similar to the one I flew on to Detroit. The only difference is it was larger. Instead of white leather, this one had burgundy leather with dark teak wood accents. The seats were double seats facing. The other side was identical. Further down the aisle were two sofas facing each other; then there was Nobody as before, seated in the left corner arms folded. It was not long before Doc came from the front of the plane, which was separated by a door with the same teak wood the plane was decorated with. Like always, Doc had this huge smile on his face as he spoke and gave me a hug. That had never happened before! He commented on my three-piece suit and asked if I had one in his size. I said no, but I ordered him four suits that would be in the store this spring. Doc said he couldn't wait and told me to make myself comfortable.

"Relax," he said. "I will be back after the plane is in the air." As he walked back toward the door, he motioned, and Nobody followed him, and they both disappeared behind the wooden door. I noticed when Doc opened the door, there was a space just as large as the section I was seated in, in the front of the plane. The flight attendant asked me if I would like something to drink before we took off.

I said no. My stomach was in knots. I needed to know why I was here. Doc had not given me a clue. The pilot made the announcement to buckle our seat belts and prepare for flight. Within minutes, we were in the air. I looked at my watch; it was 11:40 a.m., I could see my new apartment as we circled over Arlington. I thought about the fact I had not spent one night there since I rented the place. I reconsidered and asked the flight attendant for a bottle of water. We were in the air about ten minutes when the door opened, and Doc and Nobody walked out. Doc was carrying a red velvet box in his left hand and didn't waste any time getting down to business as always.

"We are flying to Los Angeles for you to meet with a guy named Cheyenne. He thinks he has been communicating with your lieutenant for the last three weeks, Nobody, and now he is ready to meet you. I need you to cut the same deal you did for Lewis with Cheyenne. You know the way I do business. It is different than these guys are used to. We never allow the product and the money to be in the same place at the same time. It's too dangerous. Cheyenne already has the sample. He's very happy with the product. He's ready to buy. But once he understands the way we do business, he may have second thoughts. The price has been discussed. It's the same as Lewis, twenty-five thousand dollars a key. I need you to convince Cheyenne the product is worth the risk. His market is about the same as Lewis's, maybe bigger. You will be making twice the money you are making now. Our deal will be the same with Cheyenne as with Lewis—two thousand for every key he buys, okay?"

I said, "Okay."

"Now Cheyenne is thirty-six, and he is going to think you are a little young and think he can take advantage of you. So if he asks your age, don't tell him you are eighteen. Tell him you are twenty-four." Doc looked over and asked, "Nobody, do you think Johnny could pass for twenty-four?" Nobody nodded his head to say yes without saying a word. All I could think about as Doc was talking was I had more money than I knew what to do with. The money was becoming a burden. He must have read my mind, because at that exact moment, he asked me how much money I had.

Before I could tell him, he said, "About a million and a half with eighty or ninety in checking. When you get to five million, I am going to show you how to move your money to an offshore account, clean it up, and make it legal for you to use. In about a year, I am going to retire, and when I retire, we all retire. You will have enough money to do anything you want to for the rest of your life. Now back to business. The meeting is at four o'clock at a restaurant he chose. A car will be waiting for us when we arrive in LA. Nobody will drive you. All you have to remember is that eyes will be on you the whole time. You have nothing to worry about." Doc opened the red velvet box, and in the red box was a gold watch and a diamond ring. "You dress the part, but you are little too clean cut for these guys. This is a Corum watch with forty-two diamonds. The only one I have seen is owned by Wilt Chamberlain. When they see it, even Cheyenne will be impressed. With the ring, all total is worth around a hundred grand. I took off my jewelry and put on Doc's. I had this unusual feeling of excitement like I was a part of a James Bond movie, but I it was no movie. These guys were dangerous. I knew Doc would never allow anything to happen to me. I knew I could trust Doc. Doc started to talk again. He was trying to make sure he had prepared me well. "You control the conversation, and you end the conversation, and do not let him dictate or demand anything, you understand?"

"Yes."

After my conversations with Lewis, I felt confident I would be okay. "I know," said Doc. "Let's have some lunch and rest before we land."

We dined on flounder and potatoes with string beans; then Doc excused himself and left me alone with my thoughts. I closed my eyes, and in what seemed like minutes, we were landing in LA. We taxied to a stop, and Doc came back to give me a heads up on his thoughts. "They may try and follow you after the meeting. If that happens, Nobody will take you to a restaurant. He knows which one. Order anything off the menu. Get up and go to the bathroom, and we will take care of it from there." Then he gave me a phone number to give Cheyenne if he needed to contact me and asked me to remember it. The flight attendant gave me my jacket but not the overnight bag. I wondered how she knew I was coming back. I walked down the stairs, and a white Cadillac Fleetwood pulled near the steps. The driver got out and gave Nobody the keys. He opened the backdoor for me to get in, and we were on our way. The Cadillac looked new, white with a white interior and a glass window that separated the driver from me, and the window was up. We exited the airport and onto the expressway when I began to notice how beautiful LA was. I had never seen palm trees before, well only in the movies. We must have driven for about thirty minutes before Nobody pulled of the expressway and made about five or six turns, and we were there. Nobody let the window down and asked me to stay in the car. He would to see if our man was there. That was the first time he had ever completed a sentence to me. I looked around and could tell I was in the hood. People were looking and smiling as they drove or walked by the car. They were waiting to see who would get out of the car. Nobody came out of the restaurant and opened the door and said he was inside at the last table on the right. When I got out of the car, I felt like every eye outside and inside the restaurant was on me. I could hear someone say, "That's the guy who played in that movie you know," and that was all I could hear, not who they thought I was. When I got to the door, Nobody opened it and then returned to the car. I entered the door, and the waitress asked could she help me. I said I was okay and walked toward Cheyenne. He was a big guy and looked like he pumped iron from the time he got up until the time he went to bed. He had more gold on than I had ever seen on one human being. He never took his eyes off me as I approached his table. I spoke calling his name as I sat down. His first word were "How old are you man?"

"What does that have to do with the price of tea in China?" I said. I had heard Bernard, Bass's partner, use this phrase. I had no idea what it meant. There was a young lady sitting at the table with him, and I could tell it was not his wife. She was closer to my age than his. But she was fine and reminded me of Simone.

"We need to talk alone," I said.

He said, "My lady stays here." I paused for about five seconds, remembering what Doc said about control.

"We talk alone, or we don't talk." That is when he took a closer look at me and everything I had on including the watch and ring. Then he told her to take a walk. She got up and walked over and sat at another table with two guys and a lady. I assumed they were all his people.

"I got the sample," he said. "I heard there was a serious connection on the east coast with the best blow in the country. When I reached out through my people to make the connection, it was like breaking into Fort Knox. I was about to give up when your man showed up and told me I had to buy at least a hundred keys a month before we could do business. He gave me a price of twenty-five thousand dollars a key. If the product is the same as the sample, I can move one hundred keys a month or more, so let's get started."

"Everything my man told you is correct, but, aw hell, here come the buts," said Cheyenne.

"Try to listen without interrupting. I don't have much time," I said. I could tell by the expression on his face, he was not used to people talking to him this way, but he had no choice. He had to respect me and what I had to say. "As I was saying, I do business a little different than anyone else in this business. With me, drugs and money are never in the same place at the same time. I don't want to put my people in danger! This is how it works. You will receive a key. It will have the name of a hotel or motel and room number with it. You will place the money in the room, come back in twenty four hours, and your product will be there. Your product will always match the cash. Don't waste time watching the room. Believe me, it's a waste of time."

"Man, is you crazy! You want me to trust you with millions of my cash? Oh, hell no! I tell you what. You leave the product, and within twenty-four hours, I'll leave the cash since this relationship is built on trust. Why don't you trust me," he said.

I told him, "I don't have to. You don't have anything I need. You see, I have plenty of cash. I tell you what. I have another meeting. Here's my number. If you change your mind, give me a call. This is how I do business. Everybody that does business with me does it this way." I was playing hard and really didn't want to leave the table without a deal. I didn't want to disappoint Doc. I moved to get up, and Cheyenne stopped me.

"Okay, we have a deal, but let me tell you this. If you ever screw me, I will find you and your momma and kill you both."

I looked him in the eyes for about ten seconds, then got up and said, "You will be getting a key from me soon." I had the same feeling I had when I came into the restaurant. All eyes were on me as I walked toward the door. When I got to the door, Nobody was there to open the door, and he rushed to open the car door before I got there. And we were on our way.

Before we reached the expressway, Nobody let the window down and said, "We were being followed. Don't look around. We are going to plan B." Without getting on the expressway, Nobody drove through neighborhood after neighborhood until we came to a main street with shops and restaurants and then pulled into a strip mall and stopped in front of this Italian restaurant called Sophie's. He got out and opened the door to the car, then the restaurant but didn't come in. A waitress seated me and took my drink order and handed me a menu. Sure enough, before she could walk away, two men and a woman came in the door. I was confident they were following me. They looked toward my table before they were seated. I placed my order loud enough for them to hear and asked where the bathroom was. She pointed and said down the hall on the left. I got up and walked in that direction. That's when a door opened on the right and someone armed pulled me into the room and said, "Let's go." I had never seen this person before, but I followed without any question. We went out the backdoor and into a white van.

"Lay on the floor," he said. We drove out of the shopping center onto the main street. "Now you can sit up," he said. I looked around and wondered whether Doc knew this would happen. I learned something very important that day: always plan as many steps ahead as you can envision when it comes to anything. After daydreaming for what seemed like five minutes, we were at the airport.

The van pulled beside the plane. I got out and walked up the steps. And when I got to the top, the flight attendant greeted me just as before, as if I were getting on the plane for the first time. She took my jacket and welcomed me aboard. Five minutes later, Nobody came aboard, smiling and sat in his usual seat. I wanted to ask him what happened when I left the restaurant, but for some reason I knew not to ask. I was offered something to drink, and this time I asked for a cold beer. "Imported or domestic?" she said.

"It doesn't matter as long as it's cold."

We sat there for about ten minutes before another car pulled up to the plane, and Doc got out. There were other people in the car, but Doc was the only one to get out. When he entered the plane, he had this huge smile on his face and sat next to me, telling me what a great job I did and how impressed he was at how I took charge. "Those guys sat there for twenty minutes before they realized you were not coming back. We all laughed"—Doc paused and said—"Cheyenne threatened you. We can't allow that to happen. We'll have to send him a message."

"How did you know what was said in the conversation?" I asked.

"The ring. It's not just a ring. It's a transmitter." He pointed to it and asked me to take it off. Doc flipped it open and showed me how it worked. "You can keep the watch. You earned it today. If we get out of LAX by six, we can have you home by midnight.

By the way, Fred was released from jail yesterday. I know Lewis will be happy."

"I am sure he will be," I said. (Two weeks later, Doc asked me to fly to Chicago on a commercial flight where Nobody met me at the airport. I put the same arrangement in place with a lady named Mrs. Willie Mae. I was surprised when I saw she was white. She looked to be in her late forties. She could have been anyone's mother. She kept calling me baby as we talked. As per Doc's instruction, Mrs. Willie Mae had no limit on the amount she could purchase). I lay my head on the pillow for the long flight home. The flight home was noneventful. We had a great dinner of steak and potatoes with green beans. After dinner, Doc retreated behind the wood door. The flight landed in DC at 11:25. Doc said good-bye and gave me my jewelry. He told me the watch he gave me was not for me to wear now. "Hold it until you can justify the cost. Talk to you tomorrow," he said. I looked over at Nobody, thinking I should say good-bye; but he was back to his old self, acting like he didn't exist.

On the way home, I called Raven. I knew it was late, but I wanted to be with her. I needed someone to take my mind off all that happened to me in just one day in the life of a drug dealer. ("You were making deals with the devil," Katy said. I said, "You're right," thinking that was the first time I called myself that word.) I needed to face the facts about my life every time I had an encounter with Doc, received the huge amounts of money I was getting almost every other week. That's what I was, a kingpin! Raven was happy to hear my voice. I could feel the excitement when I asked if I could pick her up and if she could spend the night.

"How long will it take you to get here?" she asked. "About twenty minutes."

"I will be ready." When I got there, she was waiting at the front of her apartment with an overnight bag and a garment bag hanging over her arm. After two weeks, all or most of Raven's clothes were at my apartment. We were living together. We never talked about it. It just happened. That Christmas, our sales were the best the store had ever had. Mr. Natham expressed he thought having the right inventory in stock and enough of it, made the difference. We had food and drinks upstairs for the staff. And later in the day, Mr. Natham produced a bottle of Chivas Regal and a bottle of vodka. After a couple of hours of drinking, the store was filled with the Christmas spirit. I thought this would be the perfect time to ask for a few days off. I wanted to go home with Raven and meet her parents. The store was closed on Monday the day after Christmas. I wanted to return on Wednesday. Mr Natham was happy to give me the time off. After we exchanged gifts, I rushed home to give Raven the good news, she was excited. We made plans to leave for Winston Salem, North Carolina, early the next morning.

Christmas in Winston Salem

Raven showed me this coat she wanted in the window of Hudson department store. It was a long brown leather wraparound with a fox fur collar that cost four hundred and fifty dollars. Raven was a casual smoker. I had encouraged her to quit and told her I would buy it for her if she stopped smoking. I bought the coat two weeks before Christmas and put it in my storage upstairs. I told Raven I had a surprise for her. When I returned with the box, and she saw the name Hudson department store on the box. She went crazy! She started jumping and hollering, "Is this, what I think it is?" When she opened the box and saw the coat, she put it on and danced all over the living room. Then she called her sister and told her I had bought her the coat she wanted. (Katy said, "That sounds like the coat you sent me." I said, "It was. I bought two.")

I don't think I'd ever seen anyone as happy as she was, and after living with her for two weeks, I knew it was the most expensive piece of clothing she had. I could have given her everything on her wish list and more. I was careful. I had not done anything that would have given Raven any idea of how much money I had. The "shoe boxes full of money" I put at the bottom of my closet and placed the boxes with my shoes on top. I knew she would never look in my shoe boxes. Her sister Terri called. She had decided she wanted to go home for Christmas and asked if she could ride with us. I told Raven it was okay with me. Terri's decision to go home with Raven and me made Raven even more excited, as she packed with her coat still on. I was excited too; this was my first road trip out of town since I arrived in Washington. I spoke to Mr. Natham about visiting down south as people in DC called it. Mr. Natham was from Raleigh, not from Winston Salem. I was concerned about some racist stories I had heard from people traveling south, being stopped by police for no reason except they were black and had nice cars. He assured me I would be okay.

"Just don't go any further. If you do, you will be in South Carolina, and that's the real South!" Just as Raven and I were walking out of the door, the phone rang. I told Raven to let the answering machine take the call, but she answered it thinking it was Terri.

"It's for you," she said. I said hello, all the while thinking, *Here goes my trip!*

I said hello twice before someone spoke and said, "This is Chey." I remembered the voice. It was Cheyenne. Doc told me that all his calls would be routed to me if there was a problem. "Sorry to bother you," he said. "Merry Christmas." I returned the greeting. "Hey, man, in the heat of the moment, people says things they don't mean, you know? No hard feelings!" I didn't know what to think about Cheyenne's call, but I remembered Doc saying he could not get away with the threat he made toward me and my mother, and he needed to make sure Cheyenne got the message! I could only assume the message was delivered.

I told him, "No hard feelings," and hung up the phone before he could say another word.

Raven asked, "Who was that?" Only a friend who thought he hurt my feelings. I told him everything was cool. We picked Terri up, and we were finally on our way. As we crossed the Fourteenth Street Bridge, I looked over at my other apartment and was surprised to see the entire corner units of the apartment building were decorated with Christmas lights including mine. *Someone would have to have gone into my apartment to do the decorations*, I thought. I was sure it was Shannon who took care of the decorations, because it was beautiful. I had no problem with Shannon being in my apartment. She was the one who decorated the interior of my apartment for me. The Christmas decorations looked Shannon's style. It was beautiful.

Raven and her sister were making plans to show me everything they loved about their hometown. While driving down interstate 85, I thought, *This was my first time driving long distance on the expressway.* I didn't want to share those thoughts with Raven and Terri. I didn't want them to be concerned. We drove through Richmond, Virginia, and after that, it seemed like with every mile we traveled, the sky seemed to get brighter and bluer and the weather warmer. After about four hours, we were in Winston Salem, North Carolina. I was glad when Terri and Raven wanted to ride around town before going to their home. I was nervous about meeting Raven's parents. Terri was driving as they gave me the quick tour of Winston Salem before arriving at their home. The weather was much warmer than DC, but Raven kept her coat on. Before we were completely out of the car, Raven's father came out the front door onto the porch, and before saying hello, he asked, "Whose car is this?"

Raven quickly replied, "This is Johnny's car, Dad," as she ran up the steps and gave him a big hug. He came down the steps to take a closer look at the Electra 225.

"What type of work do you do?" he asked.

"I manage a clothing store, sir."

"They must pay you well."

"They do," I said. Terri rushed up the stairs to meet her mother who was coming out of the front door with this big warm smile on her face with her arms spread wide open to give everyone a big hug.

"Mama, this is Johnny," Raven said. She smiled and welcomed me to their home. Raven had two younger sisters still at home, they came out to greet us. "These are my sisters Tracy and Pam. Pam is the baby."

I whispered in Raven's ear, "What are your mother's and father's names?"

"Helen and Bill," she said. When I walked in the house, I could smell food cooking, and it gave me the feeling of Christmas at home in Mississippi with my family! Raven's parents lived in a modest home with modest furniture. Her father worked in a tool and dye shop and her mother in a school cafeteria.

I remembered something my mother used to say. "Just because you are poor does not mean your house has to be dirty." Their home didn't have much, but it was clean. It wasn't long before we were sitting down to dinner, turkey, and dressing with all the trimmings, baked ham, chitterlings, potato salad, collard greens, macaroni and cheese, candied yams, string beans, and homemade rolls. Raven's mother was a great cook, and everything was delicious. And there was plenty for everyone to have as much as they could eat. Everyone had plenty of questions for me as we sat at the table enjoying Christmas dinner. How did Raven and I meet, tell me about your family, where does your family live, how old are you? There was one question I was glad I didn't have to answer, it was asked by Raven's little sister Pam.

"Are you rich," she asked? Helen interrupted and told Pam that was not a question she should ask. Boy, I was happy she stopped that question so I would not have to answer it; I am not sure what I would have said. I had fifteen hundred dollars in my bags and five hundred in my pocket and more money than I could count all over the place. Yes I was rich, with more money than I could ever imagine in my entire life. Yes I was rich, but I was ashamed of how I got it! Raven, Terri, and I took showers and got dressed to go and visit some of their friends. As we walked out of the house, their mother reminded us to make sure we made it back in time for church. Their family tradition was they all went to church on Christmas night. I had not been to church in a long time. I didn't know if I could face God knowing the kind of life I was living. I had anxiety just thinking about going to church, especially on Christmas night, on such a special day, "the birth of Christ." Terri wanted to get her mother a gift, so we went to a strip mall. I gave Raven two hundred dollars to buy gifts for her sisters, mother, and father. It didn't take long before she had gifts for the whole family wrapped in beautiful Christmas paper and in time to make it home for church. When we got back, Raven's father was sitting on the porch with his Bible in hand, and I was sure I smelled alcohol on his breath. Raven put the gifts under the tree and told everyone we would open them when we returned. We quickly changed clothes. I put on a three-piece suit. I had purchase three more since the first one. The weather turned cool, perfect for Raven to wear her new coat and the new dress she bought at the mall. We drove to church in separate cars; Raven, Terri, and their little sister Pam in my car, and her mother and father and Tracy in the other. The church was less than a mile from their home, close enough to walk. When we got out of the cars, there was about twenty of their extended family waiting to greet us: Raven's older sister Fay and her husband Charles, her mother's sister Tricia and husband David, who was the head of the NAACP. All the children and women were complimenting Raven on her coat like the gift was unimaginable. And I could see the men and women admiring my clothing as well. I could tell I made a good impression on her family, and all I said was hello. The name of the church was Mount Zion Baptist Church. I grew up in the church of God in Christ. we were called Holiness. This was my first time attending any other church, and I had no idea how they worship, but I knew one thing for sure: God would be there. and he knew my life and how I was now lived. In my church, we were taught that if you disappointed God, you would be punished. I wondered if the punishment would be now and what it would be. All types of things went through my head. Would God cause me to jump up and confess my sins in front of this church? Would He strip me of all my clothes and leave me naked and take away all my worldly possessions? We sat down on the benches her family sat in every Sunday. I braced myself for the punishment. The choir started to sing, and the people stood up to sing along; I knew the song "Lord, I Lift My Hands to Thee," but I couldn't say the words. The choir sang two more songs, and we sat down. The pastor prepared the church for the offering. I was sitting next to Raven, and she was sitting next to her mother and father. When the offering plate was passed to me, I put the two hundred and fifty dollars I had in my pocket into the plate. And they all looked at me with their mouths open, not knowing what to say. As the plate was passed to the usher at the end of the row, the usher took the $250 out of the offering plate before he passed the plate to the next row. My thinking was, if I gave God a large donation, He would forgive a little of what I was doing and not punish me on Christmas day. After church, Helen and her husband asked me why I put all that money in the church offering. I told them I had not given God anything in a long time, and I wanted to catch up.

Raven's father said, "I told old man Sampson to make sure those hundred dollar bills made it into the offering. I told him twice." We returned to their home, Raven and her sisters opened the presents we had purchased. Her father asked me to join him in the kitchen. He cut both of us a large piece of chocolate cake and asked me to sit down. "You do like chocolate cake, don't you?" he asked.

"Yes, sir. It is one of my favorites."

"You seem to be doing well for yourself. What are you plans for my daughter? She seems to like you a whole lot," he said.

"I like her a lot too, sir. Raven makes me happy," I said.

"I am her father, and I love her. Treat her right. That's all I ask you to do. That's a nice suit you have on," he said. "How much does a suite like that cost?"

I hesitated. "About three hundred dollars."

Her father said, "Man, alive, three hundred dollars for a suit. That's too rich for my blood. When you have to raise five girls, you find yourself paying long after they left home. Now give me the keys to that fancy car, and I'll take it for a spin."

"Sure," I said. I was not sure I wanted to, but I couldn't say no. I gave him the keys as Raven walked into the room and asked what we were talking about. "You and me and everything in between," I said. "Now your father is about to take the car for a spin."

She said, "Daddy make sure you return soon. We are going out tonight. Oh and, Daddy, you don't need to drink anymore." That statement made me concerned! Within a few hours, Raven's father was back and a little drunker than he was before he left. But the car was okay and in one piece. She said her father turned into another person when he drank. He would beat her mother for no reason. Raven looked very sad when she was telling me this. I knew it was not easy for her to talk about. She didn't want to go out because as soon as we leave, she said he would find a reason to fight with her mother. So we decided to stay in and enjoy the remainder of the evening watching television. I almost never got tired, but I welcomed some rest. Her father tried twice to start a fight that evening with her mother. He asked her to fix him some chitterlings and then complained they were cold. Terri reheated them for him, and after eating them, he just stared into the bottom of the bowl. Then he got up and went into the bedroom and called for Helen to come. But everyone in the house encouraged her not to go. After calling her three times, his voice went silent, and we could hear him snoring. I am glad they defused the situation, because I knew for sure I could not have stood idle while he beat her mother. We watched TV until it sounded off and went to bed. Raven's mother made a place for me on the couch. Somehow I knew that would be my bed. Laying on the couch, I was thinking about the Christmas day I had just celebrated. Going to church was deep in my thoughts. I wanted to talk with God and ask if he still loved me, and then I answered the question in my mind; I couldn't see how he could. I missed my relationship with God. I used to talk to him all the time. It wasn't long before I went to sleep only to be awakened by Raven on top of me. She was telling me how much she loved me, kissing me as she spoke, and before long I was deep inside her, and we were making noises I thought would wake everybody up. We tried to quiet the noise by kissing each other when we both climaxed. ("There you go with that sex talk again," Katy said.) Raven was lying on top of me and was falling asleep. I encouraged her to go back to her room. She moaned with rejection because she didn't want to go but got up anyway and went back to her bed.

I was not long after I could see daylight through the blinds. I heard her father in the kitchen making coffee. I sure was glad he didn't get up earlier. It wasn't long before the house was awake, and voices coming from the kitchen sounded like Raven's father was back to his normal self, laughing as he talked to Helen. Now it was the Monday after we celebrated Christmas, and our plan was to leave for DC around four that afternoon. We wanted to make the most of the time we had left. It wasn't long before the smell of bacon and eggs and homemade biscuits was coming from the kitchen. This town reminded me of the small town I grew up in, Leland, Mississippi. The one thing about Leland, well two things, are the cotton fields and the blacks, who lived on the other side of the track. It didn't take long for me to realize Winston Salem had its own tracks, blacks on one side of town and whites on the other. Washington was different. Blacks were everywhere. There were no tracks. I saw Helen on the porch after breakfast; she was reading her Bible; Raven told me it was something she did every morning before she went to work. She's been doing it as long as I can remember. This reminded me of my grandmother; she did the same thing. We visited a few of Raven's and Terri's friends, and now it was time to head back to Washington. When we returned to their home, her extended family had come over to say good-bye. We had a couple of hours before we were leaving, and we all gathered on the porch, and the questions started all over again, all directed toward me. Raven's brother-in-law wanted to tell me about his life in detail. He talked slow, and you had to listen closely to understand what he was saying. He worked at Hanes Mill Hosiery. He opened a record store that he operated when he got off work and on the weekends. He hoped one day to quit his job and run the store full time. He asked me to take a quick ride with him. He wanted to show me the store. To be polite I agreed. It took only five minutes, and we pulled in front of this little white building with a hand painted sign that read simply The Record Store. Inside it was about three hundred square feet, if that much. There in the center of the floor was a pot belly stove that heated the building. On the wall was pegboard with wire racks that held the albums and forty-five records, and they were mostly empty. During the short time we were there, three customers stopped by to purchase some records. He lost all three sales because he didn't have the product. I asked him how much he made in a given week after expenses. He said about two hundred dollars on a good week. "I put it back in the business. I am trying to build my inventory," he said. I wanted to tell him all the things I had learned from managing Mr. Men's and how and what he needed to do to be able to run a successful business. But for some reason, I didn't feel he would grasp the concept. But I admired him for trying and loaned him five hundred dollars to put directly into inventory. And I told him if he kept investing the five hundred dollars, he could build his inventory quickly. This huge smile came over his face as he told me how much he appreciated the loan and promised to do just that. We arrived back at the house and Helen was crying, and Raven and others were trying to console her. I asked what was wrong. She said daddy has been drinking again and being mean. I didn't ask what he had done, but I could tell he hit her mother. She was holding her face. I was angry and Terri was putting her luggage in the car as quickly as she could, crying as she did it. I could tell by the expression on her face she was not happy with her father. I saw Helen's Bible on the ground. I picked it up and took it into the house. Their father had gotten in his car and left. This was the first time I experienced someone being abused or knowing anyone that was being physically abused. I didn't know what to do, so I put some money in the Bible knowing she would find it and put it to good use. I knew the money would not solve her problem, or even ease her pain, but maybe it would add a little sunshine to her day. Everyone stood on the porch and waved good-bye as the car pulled out of the yard. Little did know. I would be calling Winston Salem home within a few months.

It wasn't long after we pulled away from the house that Terri begun shouting, "I hate him, I hate him!" I assumed she was talking about her father as she began to cry even harder; then Raven started to cry. I could tell this was the fatherly love they grew up with. Then Terri started to explain why she thought her father acted the way he did toward their mother. Their mother had a son when she met and married their father. Although they grew up together, their father never treated their brother well. Most of his young life he stayed with relatives most of the time. Their brother and father never got along. Their mother had not given him a son but five daughters. "He blames mama for not giving him a son," she said.

"Where does your brother live?" I asked. To my surprise, they said Washington, DC. "Where?" I asked.

"In Anna Costa." I told them that was where I stayed when I first moved to Washington with my sister and her husband. I eased our conversation toward a lighter tone, talking about the good food and laughing about some of the funny moments of our trip, like the time Raven's little sister Pam tried to go to the store wearing Raven's new coat, and it was dragging the ground. They told me about some things their family and friends said about me that I hadn't heard. We begin talking about other things, and it quickly diverted to all that was good about the trip. Before we knew it, we were in DC and dropping Terri at her apartment. Overall, we agreed we had a nice time. Raven asked if I would pick her up later. She wanted to stay with Terri. She could tell she was still upset, and I agreed. I was back in Washington, and my mind instantly switched back to the person who needs to be on guard, monitoring every word and every move I made. I retrieved my mail and checked in at the front desk before going upstairs. I was surprised at how many gifts had been delivered in person and by mail. I had to make two trips upstairs. There were so many, and I couldn't wait to see who they were from. Most of them were from family. All my sisters and my mother had baked and shipped my favorite cake, coconut. Doc sent a case of wine, and Bass sent a bottle of Johnny Walker Black, his favorite drink. I had gifts from people who were close to me, and some, I didn't think we were that close.

When I opened the box from Simone's parents, I had to sit down. I had not thought of Simone in quite some time. It was a surprise to receive the gift from them. It was four different kinds of preserves:—peach, plum, apple and pear—all in Mason jars just like my mother used to can. Inside was a card, which read, "God sent you when we needed you most!" I sat on the sofa and cried like a baby as I thought about Simone. I had not grieved for her, and it was all coming out now. I thought I had moved on, so why are all these emotions coming out now? Just at that moment, the phone rang. It was Raven. She could tell something was wrong. I assured her I was okay. She was calling to let me know she was staying overnight at Terri's and asked me if it was okay. "Of course. I will see you tomorrow. I may call you later," I told her. Scanning through the rest of the gifts, I saw a large box from New York. The only person I knew in New York was Barbara. I opened the box, and the most beautiful coat I had ever seen was staring at me. It was a gray cashmere topcoat with my name printed on the inside pocket. I hurried and tried it on and it fit perfectly. I put my hand in the pocket, and there was a note that read, "It reminded me of you," Merry Christmas. We carried fine clothing at Mr. Men's but nothing as fine as this. I decided this was the best Christmas I ever had. I thought of the money I sent my sisters and mother and wondering what their reactions were when they opened the cards and found the five one hundred dollar bills. I wanted to send ten times as much, but I knew they would freak out if I had. (And you, Katy, would have been waiting for me when I got home. "I sure would have," she said).

Conflicted Feelings

I noticed my answering machine was completely full. And when I turned it on to listen to the messages, the first voice I heard was Barbara's. She was in town and wanted to know if we could have dinner and left a number. I never told Raven about any of the women I dated, and she never asked. I can't explain it. I love Raven. Everything about her pleased me. so why was it when I think of the way Barbara made me feel, I wanted to be with her? I didn't love Barbara. I wasn't sure I had any feelings for her, but I loved the time we spent together. I wanted to call Barbara, but I was conflicted about my feelings. In the mean time, I listened to the other messages. The next voice was Doc. "Hi," he said, "I am going to be in Washington on the twenty seventh. Let's get together for lunch. Give me a call." He gave me the name of the hotel and the time he wanted to meet. But I didn't call him back. The twenty seventh was tomorrow. I was off and knew it wouldn't be a problem. I had gotten used to Doc popping in and out of my life without much notice. After all, he was the boss. I listened to the remaining messages of Christmas wishes from my family and friends, but I could not get Barbara off my mind. I decided to see her and had to do it without Raven knowing I was out most of the night. It was eight thirty. I needed to call Barbara and then call Raven if I was going to make this happen. I called Barbara first. She had excitement in her voice and said she couldn't wait to see me. She wanted to eat at a restaurant I had not eaten at before, Beezies.

"That is great," I said. Going to a restaurant that I frequent, I may run into someone I knew. I agreed to pick her up in one hour. She was staying at a hotel not far from my apartment, the Wilshire. It was an old aristocratic hotel where all the diplomats stayed when they came to Washington. My next call was to Raven. I laid on the bed so I could sound tired. When Raven answered the phone, her first words were "I was about to call you. I was lying on the bed with Terri, and she just fell asleep."

"She's feeling the way I feel," I said. "I am crazy tired. I think I'm going to hit the shower and hit the sack. I just wanted to check on you and Terri before I went to sleep. Did you guys eat anything?" I asked.

"No. We are going to order a carryout from the Cuban place around the corner. They are open until twelve."

"I love that place. Order enough for me," I said. "I look forward to eating it tomorrow." After love and kisses, I hung up the phone and jumped in the shower, changed clothes and was out the door. Barbara was waiting in the lobby when I arrived. As she walked toward the car, I could see every man in the lobby take a second look when she walked past. She was wearing a long gray fox coat with hat to match, a black leather miniskirt with no stockings, and black high heels. I got out and opened the door for her. She looked me in the eyes and thanked me. Smelling her perfume was intoxicating. It brought back memories of every minute I ever spent with her. When I got in the car, she pulled my face toward hers and gave me a kiss with all her tongue going down my throat. ("You are just mannish," Katy said, "too mannish. I wouldn't even listen to you if I were not so curious about what made you the man I see before me today, a man of God, who loves the Lord! How did you come so far?" she asked. I smiled and continued.) Now I didn't want to eat anything. I just wanted to have her as quickly as possible. Beezies restaurant was on Capital Hill. As I drove, Barbara's hand was rubbing the inside of my upper thigh making it hard for me to concentrate. She asked me if I had a great Christmas and what were my plans for New Years Eve.

"Christmas was the best ever," I said, "and am not sure about New Year's Eve." It didn't take long before we were at the restaurant. Beezies was a Greek restaurant. It was my first time experiencing Greek food. The doorman greeted her as Ms. Barbara, leading me to believe she had been here many times before. A young lady came from behind the counter and retrieved our coats. When Barbara took off her coat, I could truly enjoy the full view of what she was wearing. And it made me feel like the luckiest man alive. I was not really hungry for food, only to be with her! We sat down and our waiter called her Ms. Barbara. He gave me the wine menu and made a suggestion as to what wine I should order. Barbara agreed, assuring me it was a great choice. She told me later, the wine was her favorite. I was surprised to learn Barbara had ordered for us in advance. She had a special dish she wanted me to experience with her, and it had to be ordered in advance. She was sure I would enjoy it.

After explaining, she leaned forward across the table and asked me, "How did you like your Christmas gift?"

I told her it was the most beautiful coat I had ever seen. "I loved the color. It was perfect," I said. I had not bought her a gift, so I asked her what was the one gift she wanted for Christmas and didn't get.

Whatever she said, I had made up my mind I would buy it for her. She looked me in my eyes and said, "I have it now." I knew she was talking about me. We drank two bottles of wine and ate some of the best food I ever tasted: lamb shanks with roasted potatoes and carrots with fried cabbage.

"It takes two months to get a reservations here," she said, "but it was worth the wait." I agreed, looking down at my plate that now was completely empty. Barbara excused herself to go to the ladies' room. I watched every step she took to get there, and the way she walked excited me and made me want her even more.

Why didn't I feel this way about Raven, I thought. I get the same feeling but for some reason it was different. I felt the guilt of cheating on Raven, but it didn't stop the desire I had to be with Barbara. Since I have grown older, I came to realize it was only my hormones raging. I called the waiter over to request the check, only to be told it was paid for in advance. When Barbara returned to the table, I asked her about the check. She said that the dish had had to be paid for in advance. I insisted on paying for our dinner and requested the amount. She wouldn't hear of it.

"You are my guest for dinner, I invited you." As we drove back to the hotel, Barbara assumed the same position as before and began to rubbing the inside of my upper thigh as I drove. I was getting extremely excited. I couldn't wait for her keys to open the hotel door. She never got a chance to get her skirt off, or me my pants. I am not sure if we locked the door. Our lovemaking must have gone on for hours. We rested in each others embrace, and we would start making love all over again. I am not sure we said ten words to each other until we both were sure we had our fill of each other. It was three in the morning when I took a shower as Barbara slept, I kissed her on the lips and said good-bye as she gave me one last hug, never saying when we would see each other again. I left three one hundred dollar bills on the bathroom sink and a note that read, "Until next time." I drove home thinking about my evening and all that had happened between me and Barbara and wondering why I was felt guilty.

I told myself, "Raven and I were not married, so I shouldn't feel guilty." But I did. There was this feeling something was not right. I couldn't quite put my finger on why I was feeling that way. But I would soon find out why. When I got home and opened the door, Bass was sitting on the sofa having a drink and talking on the phone. I don't think he ever went home. He hung up on his call and welcomed me home.

"Did you have a good Christmas? How did you like the south?" I told him.

"I grew up in the South. About as far south as you can get, Mississippi. Did you forget?" I fixed myself a drink and joined him in the living room. Bass stated he needed me to come over and see our new apartment building. "I am having some work done, painting, and sanding the wood floors. Some parts of the kitchens needed some work. Once the work is complete we can get an extra fifty dollars a month for each unit."

"There is a large apartment that you can have," he said. "It's on the third floor. Remodel it the way you want. No rent. It's not the best neighborhood, but you can't beat free rent!"

"No, thanks," I said.

"Rent it out. We need the money. I have to run," he said. "If you have time tomorrow, I can take you to see the new apartments. Give me a call. By the way, tell Raven thanks for the sandwich."

"What? Raven? What sandwich?" I said.

"The sandwich she fixed me before you came."

"Raven is here?"

"What do you mean, 'Is Raven here'?" he said. "She lives here, doesn't she?"

"Yes, but I thought she was spending the night at her sister's."

"Nope, she is in the bedroom. See you later."

"What do I do now?" I was glad I took a shower at Barbara's, but I could still smell her perfume in my clothes! I hated lying. My grandmother said there was nothing she hated more than a liar. She said a liar could never be trusted. I went into the bedroom and closed the door softly hoping she was asleep.

As I started to take off my clothes, Raven rolled over and said, "Terri went to sleep early. I thought when you woke up you would be hungry, so I brought you dinner." I could tell she had been crying.

I told her I was not hungry. "I had dinner while I was out." I removed my clothes and got in bed, hoping she wouldn't smell

Barbara's perfume as I got close and kissed her on the back of her neck. She rolled over and kissed me the way she did before we made love. And before long, we were. I made love to her like I missed her as much as she missed me. I was trying to reassure her that nothing had happened while I was out. Afterward, I could tell she felt confident I couldn't have made love to anyone else after that performance. She didn't ask me any questions. She rolled over and told me she loved me and went to sleep. I don't think she had ever told me that before, and without thinking, I said I love you back. I think it was guilt.

Doc's Visit to Washington, DC/FDA

The next morning when I woke up, it was almost noon. I was supposed to meet Doc in one hour at his hotel for lunch. I jumped out of bed, took a quick shower, and was out the door. I got to his hotel about ten minutes late. When I walked into the lobby, Doc was seated in a chair in the corner of the lobby, talking to another man. The conversation looked serious. As I got closer, Doc got up and walked toward me. The person never looked around, but I could tell they were not pleased with the way the conversation ended. With that ever present huge smile, Doc greeted me as if he had not seen me in months. He had changed his mind about eating at the hotel. And suggested, we have lunch around the corner at a bar he thought had the best burgers he had ever eaten. I loved burgers, so that sounded great to me. While we were walking, Doc asked how I was doing and whether I was keeping my head on straight. I didn't know exactly what he meant. He quickly explained the golden rules we discussed when I first started selling drugs. I assured Doc I never once forgot what we discussed. When we got to the bar, the waiter greeted him and expressed how glad he was to see him again. He escorted Doc and me to his favorite table. It was near the back facing the door with a view of the whole restaurant. We sat down and Doc said to me, "Never sit with you back to the door. Always sit so you can see everything that going on in front of you. That's your favorite table." Without ordering, the waiter started bringing thing to our table, water, wine, and, within minutes, the biggest burger I had ever seen. Doc was right. It was the best burger I had ever tasted. After eating as much as we both could, the waiter came over and opened a box of cigars. Doc chose one, and the waiter clipped the end and lit it as he puffed hard until the smoke surrounded our table. With his head pointed to the sky, he said, "Nothing ends a good meal like a good cigar. Have one?"

"Okay," I said, having never smoked anything in my life. And as he lit the cigar, I began to choke. My eyes filled with water when the smoke filled my lungs. They both laughed as Doc took the cigar out of my hand and handed me some water.

"You are not ready for cigars, maybe in a few years." I wiped the tears from my eyes and smiled as he puffed on his cigar. Then I saw that look on Doc's face that came just before he got serious. I need you to deliver a package for me this afternoon to the FDA on Wisconsin Avenue. Leave it at the front desk for Mr. Hensley. I have the package at the hotel and another package for you. Cheyenne is moving twice as much product as Lewis. He has expanded his operation to Seattle, Washington, and as far west as Chicago."

"Speaking of Cheyenne'" I said, "I got a phone call from him just before my trip to North Carolina. He kept apologizing. What was that about?"

"I told you we couldn't allow the way he talked to you to go unaddressed. So I sent Nobody to pay him a visit. He woke up with flowers on his nightstand, with a note from you that read, 'Don't ever threaten me again. This time you get a pass.' Nobody says he sleeps with two Doberman pinchers outside his bedroom door. And when he woke up, Nobody assured me they were still asleep. To make sure he got the message. When his mother woke up, there were flowers on her nightstand, and she lives in Alabama. I would have loved to have heard him trying to explain to his mother how she got flowers from him without anyone delivering them. I am sure he was shocked to learn you knew where his mother lived. I did it that way because he not only threatened you, he threatened your family. That is why he called. You put the fear of God in his heart. Now he knows he's not in your league. Let's go. I need you to get this package there on time."

I left Doc's hotel with two briefcases: one for me and one for the FDA. I didn't see what was put in the case that was going to the FDA. But if I had to bet, it would be cash. The briefcase had a combination lock on it, and so did mine. Doc had given me my combination: 0000. And I am sure he gave Mr. Hensley his. I dropped the briefcase off at the FDA. A woman came out to retrieve it. She took the case without looking at me or saying a word. On the way back to my apartment, I saw this Chevrolet dealership with a beautiful red Camaro displayed on this elevated stand that rotated. I drove one block down the street and took $5,000 out of my briefcase and went back to buy the car for Raven. The Camaro had a list price of $4,160. It had everything including an eight-track tape player. I offered the salesman $3,850 in cash. It took less than one hour for us to close the deal. I put the car in Raven's name and bought the insurance through my insurance company. I told the salesman, I would be back to get my car and drove the Camaro to pick Raven up from work. I was three blocks away from the dealership before I realized I left my briefcase in my car and returned to retrieve it. I was sure it would not be there when I returned, not in DC! Raven got off at four o'clock, and I had twenty minutes to get downtown from Wisconsin Avenue. I made it with five minutes to spare. It was forty-six degrees, but I let the top down. People walked by wondering what climate I was in. I was parked about one hundred yards from the front of her building. And it wasn't long before I saw her walk out of her building with a huge smile on her face, as if she had seen the car. Only the car was not in her line of sight. She ran and got into a waiting car driven by a white guy. "What the hell!" I thought out loud as the car sped down K. Street.

I was having a flashback of the time I saw Simone get into that car at the club. There had to be a logical explanation. I sat there in a daze for what seemed to be hours, but it was only a few minutes. I drove the car to my apartment, rented a space from the office, and parked the car. I took a cab back to Wisconsin Avenue to get my car. For some reason, it didn't affect me the same as when I saw Simone cheating. I could only feel my heart had hardened as I was learning the love language between men and women. How naïve was I to think a woman as fine as Raven had no one in her life before me. But for some reason, I did. Maybe there was a logical explanation. I decided not to confront Raven about what I saw. Bass had explained this to me. It was to my advantage to have information on another person that they don't know you have. It keeps you one step ahead. I got back home around six, and Raven got home around seven thirty, about two and half hours after she got into the car with the white guy. I could tell she was surprised to see me. I normally got home from work around seven or eight each evening. I didn't tell her I had the day off. She said she went out with one of her friends, grabbed a bite to eat while she was out. She asked if she could fix me something. I said no. She kissed me on the lips and jumped into the shower. From that day forward, I never treated her the same way. I took her off the pedestal I had her on in my mind. I didn't ask her to leave, but she taught me something: women were better cheaters than men. I couldn't wait to get back to work. It was a relaxing place for me. It's where everything made sense.

On my first day back to work since Christmas Eve, I realized how much I missed it. Mr. Natham asked me about my trip down south and my day off. My answer was quite an experience! Then he asked to see me in his office. As we walked up the stairs, I wondered what this could be about. With my double life, it could be anything. Then he said, "Accounting called me this morning and told me you have not cashed a paycheck in two months. If you don't need the money, I can use it." He smiled. I had to think fast. I had forgotten about my paychecks. I really didn't need the money. Doc was putting money in my account from the investments every month. I had more than one hundred thousand in the bank. I told Mr. Natham I was saving the money to buy a house. That was the only thing I could think of, and the only thing I didn't have. "Good idea." he said. "Put the checks into you bank account as soon as possible. If you don't, we will have to cancel some of them and reissue you new ones."

"That would be a waste of time and money. I will take care of it right away."

"We need to get ready for the end-of-the-year sale and blow the rest of this winter inventory out the door," he said. I was so glad to be back to work. The people I worked selling clothes and making people look good made me happy. It was five in the evening one hour before closing when this guy came into the store and asked for me by name. When I came down the stairs and saw him, I was pretty sure it was the white guy I saw Raven with, but I wasn't sure until he introduced himself.

"Hi," he said. "I am Doctor Sammy. Raven's gynecologist. She told me her boyfriend worked at Mr. Men's. I have wanted to shop here for months. When she told me her boyfriend worked here, I decided to stop and look around."

One thing is for sure, I thought, *she was not fooling around. He was gay.*

"Raven and I met," he said, "when she first came to Washington. She is one of my best friends. Raven is special. You are one lucky guy." Sammy bought two suits, two shirts and ties to match. One thing was for sure, this was no coincidence, Sammy stopping by the day after I saw them together. That I was sure of. When I got home that afternoon, Raven was sitting on the sofa with a smile on her face. Raven told me one of her coworkers saw me in a Camaro with the top down waiting for her.

"Why didn't you say something?" she said. "I could tell something was wrong yesterday. You weren't yourself. Whose car were you driving?" she asked with excitement in her voice.

"Yours," I said, "but I took it back." Those words seemed to deflate her excitement.

"You assumed I was cheating, huh?" she said, now standing with her hands on her hips. Then I remembered what Doc told me when he was preparing me for this life I was now living.

"It's okay to be young," he said, "but never to be young and dumb!" I knew from months of working with Doc that a person could arrange a cover if they had enough time to make it happen. I was not sure this was the guy I saw Raven with, but it looked like him. But I gave her the benefit of the doubt. I smiled and told her I had the car in the garage. She started jumping up and down screaming and was all over me with kisses.

"Can I see it? Can I see it?"

"Yes, let me get the keys." We took the elevator down to the lobby and then to the garage. When she saw the car, she screamed with excitement. Security came in no time. I explained to them she had just got a new car and was excited. I gave Raven the keys, and she opened the door and sat behind the wheel.

"This is my dream car. Is it mine?"

"Yes, it is yours. And the title will be coming in a few days, and it's in your name." She kissed me and told me how much she loved me.

"Can I take it for a drive!"

"Sure, let me get a tape from the Electra." I grabbed the Chi-Lites, the same one I played when I got my car. We put it in the eight-track player and drove out of the garage with the Chi-Lites blasting. I don't think I had ever seen anyone as happy about anything as Raven was about her new car. We drove to Anna Costa Park and around the park twice and parked the car. Raven let the top down and back up again. It was around forty degrees outside as we drove back to the apartment. Raven dropped me off at the apartment before driving to her sister's to show her the new car. I decided not to go. I thought they should have this moment together as sisters. I went up to the apartment and ordered Chinese, later Raven returned and walked in, did a twirl in the hallway, blew me a kiss, and went into the bedroom. Shortly after, I heard the shower running and Raven calling my name.

"Could you wash my back?" she said. When I opened the shower, she had both hands against the shower wall. I knew that was my cue. We didn't make love that night. We had sex, rough sex. I don't think we ever made love again. I treated her like she belonged to me to do with whatever I pleased. Raven seemed to like the rough sex as she demanded more with every stroke. I experienced a different woman than I had before with Raven. Afterward, we were both silent for what seemed like hours before we spoke. We knew something had happened between us— something good and something bad—and we both knew our relationship had changed.

The New Year's Eve Party

When I arrived at work the next morning, Mr. Men's was bustling with sales as people were getting ready for New Year's Eve. Everyone was talking about the big party at the Fox Trap. The one hundred dollar ticket was the hottest New Year's Eve tickets and the most expensive in DC. In 1972, one hundred dollars was a lot of money! It was a black tie event. I decided to have some fun and thought carefully how I could spend some money without drawing attention to myself and came up with an idea. With some help, I thought it would work. I bought twenty tickets to the New Year's Eve party and had them delivered to my friends by courier service. Inside the envelopes were tickets and invitations to an after-party in Arlington at my new apartment. I called Shannon. I had not talked to her in a while. She was very happy to hear from me. I told her my plans to have the party at my apartment New Year's Eve, and she didn't think it would be a problem at all. I told her I needed the party catered for about sixty people. In Washington, if you invite twenty people, you can expect three times as many. I gave Shannon a five thousand dollar budget. She thought that would keep the champagne flowing and allow the caterer to offer a great food selection. I insisted no caviar and had a few other unusual requests. I needed someone to host the party. I didn't want anyone to know it was my apartment or that I was giving the party. With no questions asked, Shannon assured me everything would be taken care of.

When the tickets were delivered to the store, and to friends, everyone was so excited. And I acted excited to receive my tickets as well. Brenda and Mrs. Natham started talking about buying something new to wear. It was excitement on steroids filling the air in the whole store. The ticket invitation read: "Be my guest at the Fox Trap." It included a list of special guests at the after-party with the address to the *after* part. No one asked where the tickets came from; they were just happy they were going to the big party. I told Raven the good news and told her I had purchased a ticket for Terri if she wanted to go. And she was excited! Right away, she said she needed something to wear. I told her the event was black tie and gave her five hundred dollars to buy new clothes. Raven never asked any questions about my money. She was not inquisitive at all, and that was perfect for my lifestyle. It was New Year's Eve 1972. Raven was at the hairdresser with Terri. I was home trying on a dinner jacket and formal slacks I bought from a formal store in Georgetown that cost more than two suits at Mr. Men's. The jacket was white, and the slacks were black wool that looked like silk. The store tailored the slacks and jacket to fit me perfectly. I bought a black pair of alligator shoes that some may question how I could afford them. We made plans to leave for the party around 10:00 p.m. People who bought ten tickets or more were given a reserved table, and I had two. I put one table in Mr. Men's name and the other in Alside, which was the name of the company Doc had given me to invest in. Each table was given a free bottle of champagne.

Raven and her sister Terri arrived from shopping and couldn't wait to show me the outfits they had chosen. I knew Raven's style, and I liked it. Terri had her own hippy like style, so I had no idea what she bought. But to my surprise, she allowed Raven to influence her choice, and it looked great. With new hair styles and nails polished, they couldn't wait to get dressed. I got dressed first, so the ladies could have the bedroom. I went to the garage to retrieve the car and patiently waited for Raven and Terri in the lobby. When Raven and Terri stepped out of the elevator, they looked beautiful and sexy. I can't explain how excited they were as we drove to the club. I dropped the ladies off in front of the club and tried to find a parking space that took about twenty minutes. When we got inside, there were people sitting at our table and drinking our champagne. I asked one of the employees to check their tickets, and they were asked to move, and we were given another bottle of champagne. I quickly located my friends and asked them to join our table. I looked at Mr. Men's table and saw people sitting at their table, and I didn't recognize them. When Mr. Natham arrived he was surprised to have a reserved table in the company name, and even more surprised to find people seated at the table. I explained what happened at our table, and they were asked to move. This time Mr. Natham did ask where the table came from. I could only say I am not sure. When I looked at the two tables, they were filled with all the people I had invited. And the party was reaching high gear as the band played one hit song after the other. We danced and drank champagne until the count down to midnight. There were fourteen bottles of champagne consumed at our table that cost twenty dollars each. And no one asked where they came from. The party was filled with politicians, city officials, and famous people from television and movies. Raven and Terri were impressed and felt this was the place to be. It was the A-List party of Washington, DC, and we partied until 2:00 a.m. when people began to leave. I asked a few people if they were going to the after party and many were not sure. I was beginning to think I paid for a party that only a few people would attend. We were feeling pretty good when we left the party. I was extremely nervous about the party. I was not quite sure what to expect. As I drove to Arlington, cars were honking their horns, celebrating the New Year.

When we arrived at 1300 Army Navy Drive, I realized this was only the third time I had been to my apartment since I rented it. The water fountain in front of the building was beautiful. The colored lights made the water look red, white, and blue as the water shot high into the air. Cars were lined up as far as I could see in front of me, and behind me were at least another twenty cars. There were five men parking cars as fast as they could. I had no idea they were parking cars for my party until they parked my car. They directed us to the elevator that would take us to the eigth floor. Raven and Terri wanted to know who was giving the party. I told them I had no idea. They both commented on how beautiful and classy the building was. When we got to the apartment, there was a man outside the door who looked to be about thirty years old, dressed in a nice suit, checking to make sure at least one person in each party had an invitation. When we entered the apartment, it was already crowded. I could see everything in the apartment had been arranged to accommodate the number of people expected. A piano was placed in the corner that this beautiful lady was sitting on, singing. She had a voice that sounded like Sarah Vaughan. There were people walking around with food and drinks, making sure everyone was taken care of. This apartment was more beautiful than the last time I saw it. The lights off the interstate in the distance and from the bridge were awesome. I looked around and saw people I invited, but the others I had no idea who they were, Some of the faces I remembered were from the club. I saw Shannon, who had chosen herself to play host, which surprised me somewhat, as she chose herself. She greeted me like everyone else, welcoming us to the party, making us feel at home. It was a very odd feeling. I walked around my own apartment pretending to be a guest. I made my way to the back of the apartment where different music was playing to a different group. People filled the wraparound deck as they walked from the front and then back again. Mr. Natham grabbed my arm and started to asked me about Terri, Raven' sister. I believe it was the alcohol he had been drinking. He was holding a drink as he asked one question after another. Out of the corner of my eye, I saw Brenda from work and her crew. They were having a great time. I looked on the deck and saw Lewis with his girlfriend and Fred. I had not seen Fred since his release from prison. Lewis made a comment to me that he was sure this was the largest crowd of black people this building had ever seen at one time.

And I responded, "You could be right."

"Who is giving this party," he asked.

I quickly said, "I have no idea, some company I think." The party was loud, people were dancing, and everyone was having a good time. I found Raven talking to a man in uniform who according to Raven lived in the building. He told Raven Shannon was the building manager. And she was hosting the party for the owners of the apartment. I quickly changed the subject and asked Raven to dance. And after hours of dancing and drinking, it was getting late. I asked Raven and Terri if they were ready to leave. And it was at that very moment, the music stopped. And Shannon announced breakfast was being served in the receiving room located on the second floor. It was 5:00 a.m., and I was very hungry and very much wanted to see the second act of the show Shannon had put together. And I was not disappointed when I entered the room. Every table had white tablecloths with silverware and flowers on each table. Music was being played by a trio which was not playing at the party upstairs. People dressed in white jackets were serving pancakes, sausage, pan trout, grits, French toast, and eggs fixed any way you wanted. This was over the top! When I got a chance to speak to Shannon, I told her this was more than I expected. She said it all came in under budget. Then she informed me that my apartment was being cleaned as we spoke.

"Mr. Brown, there was money in your apartment," she said. I didn't think it would be safe there, so I moved it to our office safe. I had forgotten about the four hundred thousand I had left under the kitchen sink. I thanked Shannon for all her hard work. Shannon kept the party going through breakfast, and nobody no one was in a hurry to leave. It was seven in the morning when the lights were turned up, signaling it was time to leave. People were talking about the party outside while they waited on the valet to bring their cars.

Raven and Terri had this glow in their eyes at 7:00 a.m. as we drove across the Fourteenth Street Bridge. All I could think about was I didn't have to work on New Year's Day, and I needed to sleep. I took Terri home and waited for her to enter the building. Then my car took Raven and me home because I don't even remember how we got there. I helped Raven out of her clothes, and she fell across the bed and was out like a light. I was just as tired, but the adrenaline flowing through my body would not let me sleep. I sat on the sofa looking out of the window of my apartment, thinking about everything that happened and fell asleep. I was sleeping when I was awakened by the sound of Raven opening the door for Linwood, Sherman, and Mr. Bass while she was telling them I was asleep on the sofa.

Mr. Bass said, "Get your ass up. It's one o'clock in the afternoon," and he commented about me still wearing my New Years outfit. Raven gave me a cup of coffee and asked if anyone else wanted a cup. I noticed Raven was dressed and could tell she had plans that did not include me.

"I cooked you some breakfast," she said to me. 'But sorry, guys. I didn't know you all were coming. I am going over to pick up Terri. We're going for a ride." I was so glad she did not say in my new car. I didn't want anyone to know I had bought her a new car. "See you later, guys," and she was out the door.

"Well, that spoiled my plans," Lin said. "I came to get your car. Sherman and I were planning a trip down to Richmond and wanted to see if you wanted to ride. We wanted to take your car." I waited a few minutes before I gave Lin the keys to my car. I wanted to wait until Raven was gone. I told them Raven was driving her sister's car. A huge smile came over his face; he loved driving the Electra 225 as much as I did. This was not the first time he had driven it to Richmond. It wasn't long before he and Sherman were out the door.

Katy's Call for Help

Now Mr. Bass told me why he was here. "Let's take a ride over to the apartments you have never seen. I want your approval on some of the things I am doing." I took a shower and got dressed and took a few bites of the breakfast Raven had fixed. I glanced over at my answering machine and saw it was full. I needed to listen to my messages and clear the machine before I left. But I didn't want Mr. Bass to hear them. When we got to the lobby, I told him I forgot my wallet and went upstairs to listen to my messages. Most of the calls were from friends wishing me Happy New Year. But the call from you, Katy, was disturbing. You were crying and needed to talk. I played it twice to try to get a feel of what was going on by listening to your voice. There was definitely something wrong, and I needed to know what! I called the front desk and asked if they would tell Mr. Bass I would be down shortly. I called you, and when you heard my voice, you started crying again. (Those were difficult times," she said. I know. You told me the story of many years of physical abuse. That broke my heart. You were afraid if you stayed with your husband, you would be killed. You wanted to know if I could help you move to Washington, DC. I told you to start packing and that you would have the money within hours.

Katy had two boys, and they were both on Christmas break. I was angry and wanted to kill my brother-in-law. I had just witnessed domestic physical abuse from Raven's father and how

173

it affected them. To think my sister was experiencing the same thing had me furious! I hung up the phone and called Doc in Detroit. He didn't answer, so I left a message asking him to call me as soon as possible. Then I listened to the rest of my messages, and Doc had called, wishing me Happy New Year and asked me to call him the first chance I got. And Barbara sounding sexy, wished me a Happy New Year. I erased the message, so Raven wouldn't hear it, but my thoughts were still on the conversation you and I had just had and how to get you out of Detroit as quickly as possible. It didn't take long before Doc called me back, and I explained to him what was going on with you. I was surprised when he told me he knew. He told me when you two met. You had left an abusive relationship with your husband. He encouraged you to leave him for good, but you went back.

I looked at Katy, and she was crying, and it made me sad, so I decided to stop for the day. She turned her back to me and stared at the wall as I said good-bye. I told her I had to fly home for a few days and promised I would be back in two days.

Business kept me away for three days, and you were not happy about that. Jokingly, you said, "You finally made it back!" Some of your friends were visiting you in your hospital room. I waited for them to leave. But you wouldn't let me leave when everyone was gone. I asked if you needed to rest. "We could start tomorrow," I said.

You said, "No. I am okay. It upset me to hear you talk about my life with Rick."

"Do you want me to skip that part of my life in DC? I have been trying to tell you everything as it happened. I don't have to be so detailed."

"No, tell me everything," you said.

"Do you remember where I stopped?" I asked, checking to see if you were paying attention (Yes, Doc urged me to leave). If Rick had not been the father of your two sons, he said, Rick would be dead! Katy, you asked Doc not to tell me, so he didn't. I asked

Doc to give you enough money to leave as soon as possible, and he assured me he would take care of everything. Then he asked me to call him back. He needed to arrange a meeting. I called you back, Katy, and told you the money and a truck with two men to help you pack would be at your house soon and drive you to Washington, DC. You sounded happy and excited. Your husband was at work and was not expected to be home until four o'clock; and you thought you would be packed and on the road long before then. It was forty five minutes before I got downstairs, and Mr. Bass was gone. I wasn't disappointed. I had plenty to do before you arrived. In my estimation, it would take you about twelve hours to get to DC, and I needed to find you a place to stay. My only thoughts were to call Shannon at 1300 Army Navy Drive."

When I walked into my apartment the phone rang it was Raven; she and Terri had decided to take the day off and drive her new car home to Winston Salem, North Carolina, and wanted to know what I thought of the idea. I told her it was okay with me. I was pretty sure the idea was hatched last night at the party, especially when she said she had clothes at Terri's and was leaving from there. That was okay with me. I needed to take care of your problem and not having distractions was less stressful for me. I picked up the phone to call Shannon, not sure what I was going to tell her, and then I decided to just tell her the truth. The receptionist transferred my call to the office. I was told Shannon would be out of the office for a week, and they asked who was calling. I gave my name, and she said hold on, and then I heard a voice I had not heard since I signed my lease.

"Hello," he said, "this is Shannon's father. How can I help you, Mr. Brown?" I was not expecting this situation, so I decided to tell him the truth as well.

"My sister just revealed to me she has been living in a physically abusive marriage for a long time and has made the decision to get out. She wants to come to Washington to live for a while. She will be here in twelve hours, and I need to find her a place to live.

She has two sons, seven and nine. I know this is short notice, but I was hoping…"

And before I could say another word, he said "Say no more, Mr. Brown. We just had a three-bedroom become available this morning, and it will be ready for her when she arrives."

"Thank you. Thank you. I have one other request," I said. "I don't want her to know I have an apartment in the building." ("You had another apartment in that building?" Katy asked. "Yes.")

"Very well,' he said, "we will add that apartment to your lease. Give us a call when she arrives." I thanked him, and he asked if there was anything else. I said no, and he said, "Have a nice day, Mr. Brown," and hung up. I knew in my heart of hearts this was not the way most people were treated. It was like I had been put on this VIP list, and no one told me about it! I think of the way I was treated even today, and I miss it. Something I thought would take all day took one phone call. But it wouldn't be long before I learned the truth about my VIP status. Now, I had the rest of the day off and no car to drive. So I relaxed and watched some football. I needed the rest before going back to work, and I was looking forward to it. Mr. Men's always relaxed me and allowed me to take my mind off the complicated life I led.

Raven called to let me know they got there and how excited her family was about her new car. I could hear her family all asking to speak to me. But I only said hello to her mother. She said thanks, and she was looked forward to seeing me soon. I could tell she found the money I left in the Bible. I could hear the appreciation in her voice. Raven told me how much she missed me and when she would be home. I told her I couldn't wait to see her and to hurry back. I hung the phone up and called Doc back. I was surprised when he picked up the phone. He almost never picks up on the first call. Usually, he would call me back. We arranged to meet in Detroit in a few weeks.

"There are some changes we need to make," he said and that he would explain everything when we met. "Oh, and by the way," he said, "Katy got away just in time. Her neighbor called her husband at work to let him know what was going on. But by the time he got there she was gone

("What?" Katy said.)

"I am sure he thought I was moving across town and not out of town. She is in good hands. The two guys she is with will take good care of her."

(Katy said, "They did.")

I thanked Doc for his help and how much I really appreciated what he had done. The rest of the day I found myself cleaning the apartment, counting the boxes of money I had accumulated, which was now close to three million ("Three million," Katy said), four million with what I had upstairs in my storage. It was more money than I could spend in a lifetime. The next morning, I was at work an hour before the store opened and had it opened and ready for customers when the staff arrived. It wasn't long before I learned I was the only one who had not heard the news about Mr. Bass being arrested, I asked where and what time? "Mr. Bernard, Bass's partner, called Mr. Natham." I am not quite sure how Brenda knew. Mr. Bass was arrested on an outstanding warrant from New York, accusing him of three counts of hijacking meat trucks and racketeering. His bond was set at $100,000. Mr. Bernard said they arrested him three blocks from my apartment around the same time he left my apartment. If I had gone with him, I would have been arrested too. ("God was watching over you even though you were deep in sin," Katy said. "I never thought of it that way.")I was sure God had turned his back on me because I had turned my back on him. That was the way we were taught in church growing up.

It was now hard for me to concentrate on my work. It was not until you called me to let me know you were in Washington did I think of anything else. I told the driver how to get to the apartment building and then called the apartment office to let them know you were on the way. I told you I would be over after work. I couldn't wait to see you and the boys and thought how great it would be to have another relative living here. Every since Selenia and Richard moved to California, I felt disconnected from my family. After work, I went as fast as I could across the Fourteenth Street Bridge to Arlington in the rush hour traffic. Everyone in DC knew not to try and cross the Fourteenth Street Bridge until after rush hour, or you could be sitting in traffic forever. I didn't care. I couldn't wait to see you guys. When I got there, the U-Haul truck was still parked in the loading zone near the freight elevator, and the guys Doc sent were outside smoking cigarettes. I introduce myself and thanked them for all they had done. They wanted to know where the nearest hotel was. They wanted to spend a couple of days in Washington before they returned to Detroit. It was their first time in DC and wanted to have a little fun before they returned. I gave them directions to a nearby hotel and five hundred dollars for the hotel and return expenses. I was sure Doc had taken care of everything. I just wanted to show my appreciation.

When I saw you, you were filled with joy and excited to be in DC, and even more excited about the apartment. You went on and on about how beautiful it was ("It was beautiful," Katy said, "and they put a bed in each bedroom and a dining room set that seated six, which was great because I didn't bring any of those things with me"). You shared with me how the maintenance men in the building moved you into the apartment, and the school contact information for the boys was left on the table. There was also contact information with the names of the people you needed to call to enroll the boys for school. And all you had to do was make the appointment.

When we were through with the pleasantries, we went shopping for bed coverings, TVs, and anything else you needed. I told you Doc gave me enough money to take care of all your expenses for six months. That allowed me to spend money on whatever you needed without any questions about where the money came from. You were very happy, but I could see the sadness in your eyes when you thought about why and what brought you to Washington. I did everything to ease your pain by buying you everything you laid your eyes on as we walked through the shopping center. It took three trips to the car to bring everything up to the apartment. (We both laughed.) I stayed until the early morning talking about our childhood, your marriage, and what you wanted to do in Washington. You sold insurance in Detroit, and I was sure you wouldn't have a problem finding a job with an insurance company in DC or Arlington. I made it clear you didn't have to rush and to take some time to enjoy DC. I gave you two thousand dollars to make sure you had everything you needed.

But it was sad to say in less than two months, you were back with your husband. I learned from the boys you called Rick two weeks after you got to DC, and he was coming to visit you every weekend. Before I knew it, you were back in Detroit. I went by to visit after not being able to reach you for a few days, and you were gone. It was like you had vanished. I knew why you didn't tell me your plans because you knew I would have tried very hard to convince you to change your mind. ("Johnny, I wanted to call, but Rick told me not to. I knew I couldn't raise the boys without their father.") In less than two weeks after I returned, the beatings started all over again. Without your permission, I intervened and asked Doc to send Rick a message: "If he ever hit you again, I want him to know he would regret it and regret the day he was born." Doc delivered the message with a heavy hand, and two months later, after being released from the hospital, Rick asked you for a divorce. (Katy said, "I knew you had something to do with him getting beat up. That was the only time I ever saw Rick afraid.")

The Switch

Three weeks after, Doc requested our meeting. I met Doc in Detroit at his favorite steak house called Carl's. Doc wasted no time as he laid out in details why he thought this meeting was so important.

"We are going to make some changes," he said. "This is an election year. The product we are receiving now, that connection is going to close down in a few months. The government is cracking down hard all over the country to prevent any embarrassing events during this election that could derail the election of President Nixon. We were warned through our connection to close this pipeline for a few months. So in three months, the product will change from Thai Brown to China White. It is the same as the number 4 brown the dealers have been getting, but the color is white. Tell them it's called China White. When you meet with these guys you are going to have to convince them to stay with us through the change. Tell them if they decide not to stay with us when we switch back to brown, they will not be able to buy from us. They will receive their sample of China White before the switch. When they try it, am sure they will like the new product just as much as the brown, if not better. I think it's better than the Brown. When they receive their sample, if they have any problems, they should let you know immediately. As always, the buck stops with you! Have a meeting with your guys as soon as possible. You can call Willie Mae, but I want you to meet Lewis and Cheyenne face to face. The change will take place in about three months. I hate elections. They are never good for business."

I couldn't comment. I had no idea what effect elections had on crime or selling drugs or that the police told you when to stop selling drugs! I trusted Doc. He kept me safe, never deviated from the promise he made to me when we started this journey together. I have no reason not to trust him now. On the flight home from my meeting with Doc, I had this feeling that was becoming more and more frequent, like my soul was empty. ("It was," Katy said.) I would look at people going about their normal lives and wondered would I ever have a normal life again. Would I have a life without drugs? I wanted to pray, but I felt the condemnation that surrounded me had separated me from God. I felt ashamed to even think of God! I had this bewildered look on my face, so severe the flight attendant asked me twice if I was okay. She asked if she could get me something to drink. I reassured her I was okay, but I wasn't sure if I would ever be okay again. I felt trapped with no way out.

Before I left for my meeting with Doc in Detroit, I met with an attorney to get Mr. Bass out of jail. Mr. Bass was extradited to New York, and his bond was raised to $150,000. I told Doc what I was doing. He told me how to conduct the transaction. I met with an attorney Doc recommended and gave him $165,000 in cash for Mr. Bass's bond. Doc's position was if the attorney placed the bond, the source of the money could not be revealed. When I got home from my trip, there were two more boxes containing $500,000. It was three times what I had just spent on Mr. Bass's bond. The attorney called a few days later to inform me Mr. Bass came by his office trying to find out who posted his bond. He told Mr. Bass that was attorney-client privilege. He couldn't say. But he did tell Mr. Bass it was a friend. Mr. Bass commented, "A damn good friend!"

I met Lewis in Greenville, South Carolina, one months after my meeting with Doc in Detroit. Lewis understood how elections affected the change and commented, "Things get tight during an election year." In some cases, he said, he had seen the well run completely dry for months. He agreed to work with the China White if it was as good as the brown. I told Lewis he would get his sample in a few days and to let me know if it works. I drove for six hours to meet with Lewis in Greensville, South Carolina. I was back in time for work the next day. I arranged to meet Cheyenne in Chicago one week after my meeting with Lewis. Cheyenne would be in Chicago attending his aunt's funeral. We agreed to meet after the funeral at the repast. I flew into O'Hare Airport on a Sunday morning. I decided to get my shoes shined before taking a cab into the city. I remember sitting in the chair as this old man, who looked to be around sixty, was shining my shoes. He looked up at me as he was shined my alligator shoes and asked.

"Are you making it or faking it, Youngblood?" I told him I really didn't know. He said, "If you don't know, you're faking it." In my heart I knew he was right. Cheyenne and I sat at a table alone in a room full of people who attended his aunt's funeral. This was the first time we had seen each other since our first meeting in LA. He treated me very differently than before. He treated me with great respect. Once, I told him about the changes and the reason behind them. Cheyenne understood why the change in product was happening. He agreed to stay with me as his supplier and complimented me on making him a rich man. He commented on how he appreciated the tips I gave him that saved him and his boys. I had no idea what he was talking about, but I was sure Doc had prevented something or helped him in some way and put my name on it. My meeting with Cheyenne lasted for less than an hour. I called Mrs. Willie Mae from the reception hall. she agreed to meet with me rather than call me back on a secure line. After a thirty-minute meeting with her at the same location, I had four hours before my flight back to DC. I have family in Chicago, a first cousin and aunt. But I couldn't call them without having to explain why I was in Chicago and didn't have time to visit, so I didn't call. I befriended the cab driver that picked me up at the airport. When we arrived at the funeral, I gave the cab driver a twenty dollar tip. He asked if I needed a cab after the funeral. I will need a cab back to the airport I told him, but I have no idea how long the funeral would be. When I came out the door, to my surprise, he was waiting. I had a couple hours to kill before my flight, so I decided to do some shopping. Carlos, the cab driver, took me to Michigan Avenue. Carlos looked to be around thirty. And although I tried to act and dress older, am sure he knew I was young. But never would he have guessed eighteen. He parked his cab and went off line with his dispatcher when I offered to buy him lunch. Afterward, we walked along Michigan Avenue where I bought some men's clothing I had not seen in DC. Heavy sweaters and pants. Walking past this beautiful jewelry store, I saw this beautiful watch I wanted Raven to have. I went into the store to inquire about the watch and the sales lady acted as though I couldn't afford the price. It was a Rolex. I had never heard of Rolex. The brand wasn't popular in 1973. I just liked the watch. I asked how much. When she told me, I said I would take it, and I bought a ring I thought Raven would like as well. Carlos was smiling as the saleswoman was now calling me sir; her disposition had changed. I asked her to wrap them, They were for a very special friend. She commented, "A very special friend."

It was time to leave for the airport. Carlos went to retrieve the cab that was now about three blocks away. When he returned, he had a young man in the cab sitting in the front seat with him. He asked if I minded if he made a quick stop before we headed to the airport. I am sure he was surprised when I said yes. I did mind and told him I would take another cab. I could tell Carlos was visibly upset when I took my overnight bag out of the backseat of his cab and raised my hand to catch another cab. My plan was to give Carlos a hundred dollar tip above the cost of the fare to really make his day. But I didn't like the fact he thought taking on another passenger would be okay with me. Doc always told me that most of the bad things happen when you lose control of what's going on around you. I felt I had lost control. I was not sure. It could have been a setup, robbery, or not. I couldn't take the chance. I arrived at the airport in Washington at eight forty-five, and Raven was there to pick me up. I was happy to see her. We had not spent much time together. I had been busy traveling almost every weekend. Being apart brought us closer together. I decided not to give Raven her watch and ring. Her birthday was coming in three weeks. I chose to wait and give it to her then. That night after having violent sex with each other, I had a dream. I was being chased by two or three men I couldn't tell. I ran into this building and began opening doors trying to escape. Every door I opened, there was a person behind the door with a gun shooting at me. I closed the door and ran to the next. With the last door I opened, Doc was standing there smiling. Finally, I felt safe, but Doc pulled a gun and started shooting at me too, and I started running again. I realized I had no place to run.

I didn't tell Raven about the dream. The next day at work, I tried to make sense of the dream. That afternoon, I called Doc. He asked me to call him on a secure line. Hearing Doc's voice, I thought, would give me the feeling of security I always had when I heard his voice, but this time, it didn't. He just needed to know if everyone was on board with the changes. I told him the meetings went well and that everyone was on board if the samples were up to par. Doc said, "Great, great, great," and then said, the samples of China White had already been delivered to them. "As soon as you hear comments on the samples, I need to know." I assured Doc I would call as soon as I heard anything. On my way home that afternoon, I once again thought about the dream and how real it felt. Doc called me every day to see if I heard anything from Lewis or Cheyenne or Mrs. Willie Mae.

That was unusual for Doc to call so much. After five days, I was able to give Doc the results. They were raving about the

China White. Lewis said it was the most powerful heroin he had ever put on the streets. The dealers told him the high the users were experiencing lasted two to three times longer than the brown did. Lewis joked that he wasn't sure that was good for business. Doc was extremely happy about the results and glad everyone was on board. I don't think I had ever heard that much excitement in his voice since we started this journey together. I was happy because whenever I became actively involved was when something went wrong or had the potential to go wrong. Now my life was back to normal or what I could call normal. Things were great at the store, Raven and I had grown closer. We began to talk about marriage. That's when it all fell apart. I returned home from work one evening. I had a call from my mother. She had received a letter from the United States Army. I had been drafted! I was not even thinking about the armed forces. When I started the twelfth grade, they had recruiters at our school. I tried to volunteer and was rejected. When I was twelve, I fell on a piece of coke bottle that lodged right under my left knee cap. When I took the physical, I failed because I could not squat long enough on my left knee. By now the war was producing casualties at an alarming rate. On the evening news, every night they were showing body bags of soldiers who lost their lives in combat in Vietnam. Now men that had been rejected were being reevaluated and called into service. If I had registered for school, none of this would have happened. I told my mother to send me the papers. I felt sick to my stomach. Now that I had gotten a chance to experience life as an adult, I didn't feel the same about the war as I did in high school. On the other hand, I thought it gave me a chance to escape the life I created for myself. *Was God giving me a way out?* I thought. I was sure God stopped thinking about me long ago.

I sat in my chair in the living room waiting for Raven to get home so I could tell her I had been drafted. I wasn't sure how she would react. I decided to call Doc first. I left him a message to give me a call and that it was very important. Within twenty minutes, he called me back. He sounded anxious to know what was wrong, asking me twice what was wrong before I could answer.

"My mother just called to inform me I have been drafted," I said. I could hear the relief in his voice as if what I told him was not what he was expecting.

"Tell your mother to send the papers to this address and not your address. I will take care of everything. I know what to do. Just have her send me the papers." Doc gave me the address. In the last eleven months, I have seen and heard some amazing things form Doc, but this was the government. What could he do? "Do not tell anyone else you were drafted," he said. "Is everything else okay?" he asked.

"Yeah, everything is okay."

"Stay in close contact with Lewis and Cheyenne and Mrs. Willie Mae. If they have any problem with the new product I want to know right away!"

"Okay." Doc had never asked me to stay in touch with them before. This was the first request of this kind. I liked the hands-off approach. *It worked well so far. Why change it now?* I thought. I hung up the phone. Raven walked in the door. I had to act as if nothing was wrong, although a few minutes ago my life had fallen apart. I called my mother and gave her the information Doc had given me. I told her to make sure she mailed it to that address and not mine. Three weeks later, I asked Doc about my draft status. He told me as my personal doctor my health condition would not allow me to serve in the military. Therefore, your military status had been changed. I never heard from the army again. I was relieved but yet sad. God had not given me a way out. And if he did, I am not sure that was the one I wanted. Doc was asking every week if everything was okay. I told him it was. I was not checking with Lewis, Mrs. Willie Mae and Cheyenne as Doc had requested me to do. I had no reason to. If there was a problem, they would contact me.

Methadone

That's exactly what happened two months later. I received a call from Lewis at two o'clock in the morning. It had been exactly three and half months since the change to China White. He said, "We need to talk. I think it would be in your best interest and mine if you didn't tell anyone we talked. I need you to come to Atlanta as soon as possible. Give me a call when you are on your way."

Lewis hung up the phone without saying another word. *What could this be about?* I thought, going to Atlanta without Doc knowing could be dangerous. Lewis and I had developed a relationship. I felt like I knew him well, but how well do I know him? Was it enough to trust him with my life? I couldn't go back to sleep. I decided to trust Lewis. When I got off from work the next day, I went home, got my car, and drove to Atlanta without telling Doc or Raven. I would keep the meeting between us as Lewis had requested. I knew I was putting my life in Lewis's hands. If I made the wrong decision, I might not be coming home. I arrived in Atlanta at 2:30 a.m. without telling Lewis I was on the way. I called him from the White Castle off I-85 to tell him I was in town. I left a number for Lewis to call. Thirty minutes later, Lewis called. I told him where I was.

"I will be there in thirty minutes," he said. If he would have made any excuse not to meet me because of my surprise arrival or if it was more than an hour before he could meet me, I would have known that it was an attempt on my life. I would have been back on the road to DC. Lewis arrived in less than thirty minutes and sat down across from me. He said to me, "Your being here tells me what I needed to know. That is what I am about to tell you, you didn't know what was going on."

I was confused. "Didn't know what?" I asked.

"I was concerned about the China White," Lewis said. "I have been for the last months. My dealers started telling me about the slow return of their buyers. It didn't bother me at first, but a couple of weeks ago, one of my dealers saw one of his best customers that told him something strange, that the China White helped him kick his habit. I asked him to bring this guy to me; I wanted to talk to him. When I questioned the guy, he said after a few moths on the white, he didn't have the desire for heroin. That was confusing. So I had a friend that works for the CDC here in Atlanta test a sample for me. She called me yesterday, nervous as hell. I met with her to see why! The China White we have been selling is pure methadone. Without a doubt, pure methadone. Johnny, this shit is government controlled. We are all dead men when this experiment is over. I just got a new shipment. I took it to buy some time. If they don't know we know, we can plan an escape. But you and I know you can't run from these folks. I have always been suspicious of you and the whole thing. The brown thing we were getting from you, only three people had it in the whole country. That's why I could move a hundred to a hundred fifty keys a month.

The China White has slowed sales to a snail's pace, and all the dealers were puzzled. Now I know why, and now you know why. I asked you to keep this meeting between you and me, because the people you are dealing with know what's going on. And at some point, they knew we would find out. That time is here my friend. What do we do now? I thought you were behind all this shit, but I have known from the start. You were the front man. You are being used right along with the rest of us fools. The person that works at CDC that gave me this information is family. I don't want anyone to know how we found out. I don't want their life in danger. I don't know if you told anyone about this meeting. You said you didn't. But if I get home, and you get home alive. I know you are telling the truth."

I watched as Lewis walked out the White Castle. When he exited the door, Lewis held both arms stretched open like the crucified Christ and held the position for about ten seconds and then walked to his car and drove off. That would be the last time, I would see Lewis alive! I sat there trying to digest what Lewis had just told me. What in the hell is methadone, and what do I do now? My exiting the door could be the end of my life if Lewis felt this was entirely my fault, and he would be right. It was. I got up from the table, paid the check, and walked to the door, hesitating before I opened it. And did the same thing Lewis had done. I opened my arms wide standing there for what seemed like forever before I got in my car and headed back to DC. I had no idea what to do once I got back to DC. Like Lewis said, "We had some time to figure out if anyone knew we knew what was going on." I kept wondering if Doc knew. He must know. Now it is all very clear to me. From the beginning, this show has been directed like a broadway play. Every piece perfectly placed for it all to work. Lewis had given me a lot of information, but my question was, why? I heard of methadone on the news. It was a drug treatment program put in place in different cities across the country to help war veterans and others hooked on heroin and other drugs to kick the habit of addiction. I was pretty sure Doc's insistence I check on Lewis and Cheyenne and Mrs. Willie Mae was because he needed to know if the operation had been exposed. I had not called Doc. I hoped he wouldn't call me. I had never lied to Doc, but it appears Doc has been lying to me all along. For the next few days at work, I was a zombie. Mr. Natham asked me if I was okay more than once. I told him on the third day, I felt I was getting the flu.

He said, "Everything around here is going well. Go home and try to fell better. We can do without you for a few days." Walking from the store to my apartment, I am sure I looked over my shoulder a hundred times before I got to my apartment. I closed the door to my apartment, and I felt something I never truly felt before; fear! It had been over a week since I talked to Doc. I was glad I had not spoken with him, but once a week, he was calling to check on Lewis, Cheyenne, and Mrs. Willie Mae. Why haven't I heard from him? "Without any evidence," and Lewis's word only I decided to confront Doc. The next morning, I called him not quite sure what to say other than, "Are we selling methadone, and why?

When I called Doc's number, the operator came on the line and said, "The number you dialed has been disconnected. Please check the number you are dialing, and dial again." I was sure I dialed the right number, so I dialed it again only to get the same message! This could suggest only two things. What Lewis told me was correct, and we don't have as much time as we thought to plan our escape. Maybe I thought Doc had changed his number and there was a good reason he had not told me. I stayed out of work for three days, never leaving the apartment. I was playing sick. Raven was concerned and wanted to stay home with me. I convinced her I was okay. But it was time to return to work. I didn't tell Raven what was going on because I wasn't sure what was going on. I tried to act cheerful at work, but if they looked really close enough, they would see I was still dealing with the mess I had made of my life. I tried to call Doc once again with the same result, the number was disconnected. The day I returned to work, I decided to go to happy hour after work with the guys, something I had not done for sometime. I thought it would take my mind off the thoughts running through my head every second. But it didn't. I had only one drink' I wanted to stay sober and alert; I was trying to convince myself that what I was concerned about was all to do about nothing.

The Death of Lewis

Jimmie, one of the salesmen from work, gave me a ride home. When I arrived at my apartment around ten o'clock in the evening, I walked into the lobby. Out of the corner of my eye, I saw what looked like Fred. And with a quick second look, it was Fred. I had not seen Fred since the New Year's Eve party. Fred was Lewis's enforcer. He was sitting in the lounge area when I walked in. When he saw it was me, he got up and walked toward me, and when he was close enough to speak, he asked if we could talk. Whenever Fred showed up, someone was seriously hurt or killed. But I knew if Fred wanted me dead, he wouldn't have shown up in my lobby. Just to be safe, I didn't invite him up to my apartment. We sat in chairs, facing each other when this look of regret came across his face, and then he said. They found Lewis dead this morning in his apartment in New York along with his girlfriend, Linda. Lewis was tortured before he was killed. His fingers and big toe were removed, his eyes punctured out. Linda was shot in the head while she was still sleeping. There was no sign of forced entry. It was not a robbery. Lewis had a half a million in cash in his closet. I am sure whoever did this to Lewis either knew him, or they were able to get into his apartment while they were sleeping. Lewis was a pro at staying one step ahead of the game. He moved every six months, never staying in one place too long. Lewis would have never let his guard down for someone to get this close. Lewis told me everything that was going on.

"My question to you is, do you think your people did this?" While Fred was talking to me, it was like he was talking in slow motion. I was still on his first words: Lewis was found dead this morning! He called my name three times before I said a word. I am sure I fainted. If I would have been standing, I would have hit the floor.

"They found him this morning?" I asked.

"Yes, they estimate they had been dead at least two days."

"Do you think your people did this? I am beginning to think Lewis was right," I said, "and we are all in trouble. Fred said he thought I was in danger."

"I can take care of myself," he said. "But you, on the other hand, probably don't even own a gun. You are not safe here. You need to move! Do you have a place you can go," he asked, "a place no one knows about, not even your best friend?"

"Yes!"

"If I were you," he said, "I would not spend another night here. It's not safe." I got the feeling Fred always had someone to take care of, and now Lewis is gone; it looked like he adopted me. I know that Fred loved Lewis. I have seen them interact many times. If there was anything Fred could have done to protect Lewis, he would have done it. Fred would have given his life to save Lewis. I'm sure of that. Lewis stretched Fred too thin that's why Fred was not there when he needed him the most. I didn't know who to trust. I couldn't trust anyone, but I did give Fred Cheyenne and Mrs. Willie Mae's number and asked Fred to warn them and anyone else he could think of who might be in danger.

"Give them as much information as you can about what is going on and tell them to do whatever they can to protect themselves." I went upstairs and woke Raven. I told Raven to pack some clothes as fast as she could and that we need to leave the apartment. Without any question, she started packing. I put a few things together and took all the money I had in the apartment and left the money and Lewis's jewelry He had given me to keep in the storage upstairs. We took the elevator to the basement and packed the things we had in Raven car as Fred stood watch. I gave Fred the keys to the storage and the Electra 225 and told him about the money and the jewelry in the storage unit upstairs. "Take care of it. We may need it later," I said. Raven and I drove toward Virginia on I-95. I made sure no one was following as I drove to the apartment in Arlington. I passed Arlington like we were leaving town, headed toward Alexandria. When I was sure no one was following us, I came back to Arlington on a two-way street through Alexandria. I told Raven as much as I could about what was going on. I explained to Raven that people were dying around me, and I didn't know who was responsible. I couldn't tell her everything. I didn't want the information I told her to be used against me later. I was still thinking the way Doc had taught me. I was now thinking, he is behind Lewis's and Linda's deaths, and I could be next!

When we arrived at the apartment, Raven gasped for air and said. "This is the building where we went to the New Year's party."

"Yes, I gave the party," I said.

"You?" she asked.

"Yes, me. I wanted to have a party and didn't want anyone to know I was having the party. Does that make any sense?"

"Yes, now thinking back on everything, it does!" I parked the car in the garage. We took the clothes we had and the money she didn't know I had, and we went upstairs. Raven was so excited that the apartment was mine. She forgot the danger I had just shared with her as she looked in every room! I had some clothes at the apartment. I was not sure what Raven had brought. I explained to Raven that we should continue with our lives as if nothing was wrong, until I could figure out what was really going on. I suggested that Raven stay with her sister until I was sure she would be safe with me, but she said no. That night, Raven slept in my arms all night. I wasn't able to sleep at all as I thought about Lewis. He always thought he could hide in New York among the millions and be safe. I remember him telling me Fidel Castro could hide in New York, and no one would recognize him, and now Lewis is dead. Whenever I had time to think, I wished I could talk to God about what was happening to me and the mess I had made of my life. My grandmother told me when we would spend time on the porch together the times I would visit her and my grandfather in Crystal Springs, Mississippi.

"This is how we are made," she would say. "We are spirits, we have a soul, and we live in these bodies. God created these bodies for us to survive in this environment. We are made like God. We are spirits. Always follow your spirit," she said, "and always talk to God." That's what I missed the most in my life, the way I used to talk with God. I felt so alone!

The next morning, I suggested we take the bus into the city. There was a bus stop in front of the apartment building that would take us to downtown DC. I thought if we didn't sit together, it would be safer. When I got to work, Brenda couldn't wait to see me. She was crying, and everyone was talking.

"Did you hear about Lewis?" she asked.

"No, what about Lewis?" I said. "He was killed in New York." I tried to act surprised.

As I walked upstairs toward my offices, I could hear Mr. Natham saying, "You live by the sword, you die by the sword." ("That's right," Katy said. "I always felt creepy around Doc. I never trusted him. That's why I broke it off with him.") Mr. Natham stated we had received about 80 percent of our spring and summer orders. He informed me that Doc's order was almost complete. I was happy we had not received Doc's complete order. If Mr. Natham would have asked me to contact him, it would have put me in an awkward position. Being at work, going about my everyday routine, took my mind off my troubles. I felt safe there. Raven was calling every hour until I told her to stop. Mr. Natham was asking if everything was alright with her. Then she would call every two hours. Brenda was crying uncontrollably, so Mr. Natham gave her the day off. I found myself daydreaming about the times Lewis and I were together and the first time we met. I could still see his big smile and those steel blue eyes. I couldn't believe he was gone.

I couldn't remember the last time I had eaten anything. I was hungry, but I didn't have an appetite. I knew I needed to try and eat something. I had not left the store all day. I was apprehensive about walking down the street. I was afraid. The Blue Mirror restaurant was directly across the street. I decided to go over there. I loved their opened-faced hot turkey sandwich with cranberry sauce and gravy. When I walked in, the place was crowded. I felt safe among so many people. I moved three times before I settled in a booth near the front. I wondered if anyone noticed my behavior. I was not seated five minutes before Fred came in the door.

"They told me at the store I could find you here," he said. "I called the number you gave me for Cheyenne, and this lady answered the phone," she said. "She was Cheyenne's niece. Get this, Cheyenne was killed this morning in a car accident. A tractor trailer ran a red light, killing him and two other people. Johnny between you and me, I don't think it was an accident, and get this, Frank's wife in Philadelphia said he left the house two days ago, and she has not heard from him since. That is not like Frank. The only thing that would keep Frank from calling home is if he couldn't. I didn't think you needed to wait to get this information. You need to go underground as quick as possible. These murders are no coincidence. Somebody is cleaning up their mess. I got the money from storage, and I will keep it until I hear from you."

"Fred," I said, "if anything happens to me, make sure my family gets more than enough money to bury me. Make sure my mother and Raven are taken care of."

He said, "You got it! Listen I have a gun. You want me to leave it with you?"

"No, I'll be alright." Fred got up as the waiter was bringing my sandwich to the table. I ate a couple of bites. The food felt like cement going down my throat. I don't know how long I sat there staring at my plate, but the lunch crowd was all gone when I realized I was the only one left. I put ten dollars on the table and walked back to the store crossing four lanes of traffic without looking either way.

Visit from the DEA

When I walked in the store, I saw two men in suits standing at the bottom of the steps that lead to the upstairs offices. Looking upstairs in Mr. Natham's window, I could tell there were men in suits upstairs with him. One of the men walked toward me and asked my name. When I told him, he reached out and gently put his had on my forearm and said I was needed upstairs, as Mr. Natham and the two men looked out of the office window.

My head was spinning. *What is going on?* I thought. I came to the conclusion they wanted to talk to me about Lewis's death. When I entered the office, Mr. Natham said these officers are from the DEA, and they just told me some things that I have a hard time believing.

Then the large man, about six foot six, said, "Maybe you should sit down, Mr. Brown. As Mr. Natham said, we are from the DEA, Drug Enforcement Administration. We have evidence that we gathered during our investigation that leads us to believe you are one of, if not the largest, drug dealers in the United States." Chills came all over my body, and I started sweating at the same time as the officers laid out pictures before me showing me in meetings with Lewis, Cheyenne, and Mrs. Willie Mae as well as a voice recording of my meeting with Cheyenne. That explained the jewelry Doc gave me before the meeting. They recorded every word. I felt like a caged animal with no way out. Then the officer said something very shocking to me and, I know, Mr. Natham!

Now the officer said, "You can leave the Washington, DC, area, and I mean the area, and we will not put anymore resources into bringing you to justice! If you are in the area in forty-eight hours, we will bring you to justice, and your ability to accept this offer will be off the table. Do you understand?"

I dropped my head as to say yes. They nodded their heads at Mr. Natham and said good-bye. I watched them walk out of the door. Five men dressed in gray and blue suits in single file as the staff whispered to each other. Mr. Natham sat behind his desk with his legs crossed and his hands on his knees. I could only say how sorry I was to Mr. Natham and thanked him for everything he had done for me. He bowed his head just as the DEA officers had done, as to say good-bye without saying a word to me. I went across the hall to my office, took a few personal things I wanted, and put them into my briefcase.

I could hear Mrs. Natham going into Mr. Natham's office and closed the door. I heard her scream, "What the hell! Are you serious!" I walked down the stairs and out the door. Not looking anyone in the face, I couldn't bring myself to look back; I felt so ashamed. I knew I had let Mr. Natham down. He trusted me and loved me like a son. I knew I had greatly disappointed him.

While I walked down F. Street toward Fourteenth Street to catch the bus home, I realized a lot of my questions had just been answered. I knew why I wasn't dead. They needed to discredit me by exposing me as a drug dealer. Unlike Lewis and Cheyenne, there would have been many questions surrounding my death. And I knew why they didn't arrest me. They wanted me dead like the others. I knew just how long I had to live: forty-eight hours! I was sure they knew where I was staying. I had taken the new watch Doc had given me to the new apartment. I had to make plans to die! The thought of dying made my body feel like it was frozen. I knew this was my punishment for the sins I had committed. Although I had no knowledge of the conspiracy that I was a part of, I felt responsible for all the people they had killed.

Now it was my time to die. I took the bus to Arlington to my apartment where I was met by Shannon in the lobby informing me my lease was cancelled. She said they had reason to believe I was involved in illegal activity. The notice gave me forty-eight hours to vacate according to the paper she placed in my hand. The CIA had taken me off the VIP list. What a coincidence. When I opened the door to the apartment, it was virtually empty. The only things in the apartment were the things I had purchased. They removed all the furniture that was placed in my apartment. The money Shannon had taken out of the apartment before the party was sitting on the kitchen counter. I sat in the only chair in my living room staring out at I-85 as the cars passed going north and south and wondered if anyone in the whole world could be in the mess I was in. I concluded I needed to prepare myself, mentally and spiritually, to die. I wanted to ask God to forgive me. But I did not think of a forgiving God, only the God who punishes. I waited for Raven to get home as I packed her belongings. She had no choice this time. She needed to get herself far away from me as possible. When I finished packing her things, I called as many of my friends as I could to tell them the news they were sure to be hearing very soon. Knowing "they" were listening to my calls, I wanted them to know that none of my friends knew anything about what I was doing. I didn't want anyone else to lose his or her life because of me. The first call I made was to Mr. Bass. When he answered the phone, he already got the news. I was too late. Mr. Natham had already called and given him the news. I told Mr. Bass the news he heard was true, and I was sorry I had deceived him and so many others who had trusted me.

Mr. Bass said there was more to the story than I was telling him. "Let's meet and talk."

"No!," I insisted. "There was nothing left to add to this story. It's all true."

"Let me ask you this," he said. "Did you put the money up for my bond?"

I hesitated and said, "Yes, I did."

"How will I be able to get in touch with you?" he asked.

"Mr. Bass, it's best that you don't." I hung up the phone. My calls to everyone else was pretty much the same. The news was spreading fast. Everyone had heard that I was the largest drug dealer in the country. The move they made to discredit me of who people thought I was, was working. Raven called and said she called Mr. Men's and was told I no longer worked there. I told her I would explain it all to her when she got home.

She said, "I am coming home now" and hung the phone up before I could get in another word. She took a cab from DC to Arlington and came upstairs to get enough money to pay the cab fare. 'Are we moving again?" she said, looking down at the bags packed on the floor. "Where is the furniture! What is going on?"

"Sit down," I said.

"I quit my job," she said before I could speak.

I looked Raven in the eyes and said, "Raven, if you could live anywhere in the world, where would you choose to live?"

Without hesitation, she said, "Winston Salem." I was not surprised. I knew she loved Winston Salem. It was her home. Her family was there.

"I want you to leave today," I told her. "I will join you in a few days." She didn't put up much of a fight or ask many questions. I gave Raven enough money to last most people five years and asked her to find a place for us to live that we could enjoy.

"What about the danger you thought you were in?" she asked.

"I was able to get some knowledge about it today. I know what is going on. I will make sure everything is taken care of before I come to Winston Salem. All of our furniture will be shipped down to you in a few days, so you have to find us a place quickly."

I knew I was making plans for her only, but there was no way I could tell her what was really going to happen to me. I knew I couldn't take a chance with Raven being with me another night. I thought they gave me forty-eight hours, but I would hate to have underestimated, and she was with me when it happened. I couldn't take that chance. Raven and I spent the next few hours, making love and talking about our lives in Winston Salem, making plans I knew I wouldn't be able to keep. This moment, this time with her, was my good-bye, and I tried to make it special. She was happier than I had ever seen her. She was glad to be moving home with the man she thought would be her husband. I felt if she decided to leave Winston Salem after my death, she could move any place she wanted. I knew I needed her as far away from DC as possible. Raven called her sister and told her about our plans to move back home to Winston Salem. Terri had a ton of questions and wanted Raven to stop by her apartment before leaving. We had about three or four good-byes before she left for Winston Salem around seven o'clock that evening. I stood in the parking lot, waving good-bye as she backed the car up and gave me one last kiss. I watched as she drove down 1300 Army Drive until she was out of sight.

I rushed back upstairs to make more call to my family. When I called my mother, she could tell something was wrong and insisted I come home right away. I tried and failed to reassure her I was okay. I don't remember anything I said that would have indicated trouble, but she knew. ("She called me asking me if I knew anything about what was going on with you," Katy said. "This is why I needed to hear this story. Johnny, this is all surreal.") I hung up the phone and began to cry for the first time in a long time. I felt my soul crying out for an answer as I thought about the choice I made when I faced the fork in the road and wished I could make that choice again. After an hour of feeling sorry for myself, I called Carl Hayes. Hayes was a friend I met at Selenia and Richard's house when I moved to Washington, DC. Hayes had served ten years in the air force and resigned to take a job with the US Postal Service to complete his service with the government. I had talked to Hayes a few days earlier and knew he was waiting for his position to become available and needed money. I explained to Hayes why I was calling, and he agreed to take my furniture from both apartments to Winston Salem for a thousand dollars plus expenses. He had two guys he needed to help and needed three hundred for each of them. I agreed with the price and to meet him in thirty minutes and give him the money and the keys. I knew I could trust Hayes and knew he would keep his word and make sure the furniture got to Raven. The next morning, Hayes arrived at my apartment as promised and had already removed the furniture from the Washington apartment. And it didn't take long for him to remove the belonging from the Arlington apartment. It was close to noon when he loaded the final pieces on the truck. I gave him the phone number to Raven's mother's house so he could contact Raven once he arrived, and Hayes was on his way. I called Fred and asked if he would bring my car to Arlington. He arrived not long after Hayes left. He remembered the building from the New Year's Eve party but didn't comment further. He was hearing the rumors that everyone was hearing and came to the same conclusion I did. They needed to discredit me before they killed me. He wanted to know what my plans were. I told him I didn't think running would do any good! Fred agreed, gave me a bear hug, and said, "I will see you on the other side."

"Oh by the way," he said, "they found Mrs. Willie Mae at the movie theater, dead. Heart attack. But you and I know the real deal," he said.

It had been twenty-four hours since my meeting with the DEA, and I knew my time was running out. I went upstairs and got all the money I had and put it in the trunk of my car. I had no idea what to do with it. I thought of a few things I would like to do before I died. I decided to take a ride to my favorite restaurant Anna Maria's. I was at peace with what was going to happen to me, but I was still afraid! I ordered four different dishes and ate a bite or two from each one, then paid the check and walked out. The waiter asked if I was a food critic. I smiled and said, "No. I just wanted to taste my favorite dishes one last time."

The Compound

I drove to my favorite park, East Potomac Park, and sat on my favorite bench and looked out into the water. As I sat there, I was hoping this would be the place where it would all end. I sat on the bench quietly looking out into the Potomac as my life and memories of my life flashed before my eyes. I thought about the good times in my life, before Doc and drugs. For some reason, a particular time in my childhood came to memory. It was as if it was put into my subconscious. I was ten years old and was very sick and not expected to live. My mother had taken me before the elders of the church to pray for me. Everyone claimed they had a home remedy and an opinion as to what was wrong with me. My heart felt like it was going to explode at anytime, and the pain was constant. My mother would come home from work each day for lunch to rub some type of horrible smelling ointment on me that smelled worst than I felt. Later, she would have one of my siblings stay home with me each day. After a week or two, I was home alone. I was sure I was going to die, and I prayed to God each day to save me before my heart exploded. One day, I was at home alone praying, and this light came through the window, and I heard a voice speak to my spirit, which said, "Go sit on the edge of the porch facing the sun." I was weak and hardly able to walk. But I made it to the porch and sat on the edge facing the sun. The sun shined on my body. The light was the most beautiful thing I had ever seen! Some force gently closed my eyes, so I couldn't look at the bright light as it filled me with energy that felt like warm water running through my whole body. It only lasted for a few seconds, but I wanted it to last forever. When my mother came home that evening, I was playing in the front yard. She dropped the bags she was carrying and put her hand over her mouth!

"What happened?" she asked. I told her, and she called everyone from the church and told them about the miracle. Thinking about that moment allowed me the courage to pray once more. This time I felt like it was okay. I remember asking God to let my death be quick and painless. I didn't want to be tortured like Lewis. I wanted to ask God to save my life but felt as though it was too much to ask after all I had done.

While I sat there looking at the water, the number my brother-in-law gave me when he moved to California months before kept popping in my head. I remembered what he said when he gave it to me, that if I ever needed help call this number. He and my sister Selenia were concerned about me being alone in Washington. I decided to call the number and looked around for a pay phone. I spotted a phone less than ten feet in front of my car. I sat on that bench many times and never saw that phone before. While dialing the number, I was thinking of what I was going to say when a man's voice came on the phone and said hold on. After a few minutes, he came back on the phone and said, "Hold on. Don't hang up." The next time he came on the line, he said, "Hang up and call back in thirty minutes from the same phone and hung up. I looked at my watch. *It was 2:37 p.m., and I needed to call back at 3:07,* I thought. Waiting for the time to pass seemed like forever. I looked at my watch, It was 3:01 when I saw a van speeding toward my location, and before I could react, it was in front of me. The doors flew open, and two men jumped out and told me to get in. The time had come, and I didn't resist. They scanned my body with some type of device. I had no idea what it was. Then the man to my right went into my pocket and took my keys and threw them to another man who jumped out of the van, and they closed the doors. I counted four men with muscles like the men who worked in the forest where my grandmother lived. She called them lumberjacks. They slipped a hood over my head and sped away. I could feel one man's body close to mine. Silence filled the van. Even under these conditions, I was calm. I still felt the peace I had before I got the courage to call the number. I was thinking I will never know if those guys I called could have helped me. I was only seven minutes from finding out. I could tell from the turns the van made we were headed out of DC. I could hear the sound of the bridge and the sound of cars passing on the expressway. I wondered if I would ever see light again. I felt chills all over my body as I waited for the end to come. After driving for what seemed like hours, I could feel the van leave the paved road and the sound of gravel being crushed under the tires. We drove about five minutes before the van came to a stop. I heard the door open as the man sitting next to me grabbed my arm and pulled me out of the van. Each step I took felt like it would be my last, and after walking a few yards, I was placed in a chair and the hood remove from my head. I could see we were in a completely remote place that looked like a compound or school of some kind. It had lots of little houses that reminded me of the house I grew up in Mississippi but smaller. Separated from the others was a huge main house. The grounds were well kept with a view of the Potomac you could barely see through the trees. The four men that picked me up were now two. The other two men went into the large house and returned with a man dressed in a military uniform and a red beret on his head. His sleeves were rolled up close to his shoulders. He was built like the four men who picked me up but bigger. His face looked like it was chiseled out of stone. If you got in a fight with this man, you knew you were going to lose. The peace I felt had now left me and the fear returned. He walked around the chair where I was seated one time and said with a loud voice, "How did you get this number? Tell me quickly, young man. You don't have much time!"

I thought, *These are the people I called. I got through. They asked me to hold on and then told me to hang up and call back from the same number. They were pinpointing my location.* I answered, but I could barely hear my own voice, "My brother-in-law, Richard Johnson, gave me the number." I was almost crying, my voice trembling. He told me if I ever needed help to call this number.

"Richard Johnson gave you this number?" he asked.

"Yes," I said.

"Why do you think you need help, son?" I began to tell him my story. I started from the beginning, trying not to leave anything out. As I told the story, I could see them looking at each other as if they had heard many stories like mine before. When I finished, the man in the military uniform told the other men to put me away while he checked my story. Two men grabbed me by the arm and took me to one of the small buildings. One of them opened the door and gently pushed me inside as I heard the door lock from the outside. The room had a bed, a table and chair with a ceiling fan that made a clunking sound, with a small bathroom attached. Nothing fancy but extremely clean. There was a small window facing the Potomac with no glass. Being behind a locked door somehow made me feel safer than I had felt in days. Somehow knowing I was not in the hands of the men who were going to kill me, I was somewhat relieved. But I really wasn't sure what was going to happen. Later that afternoon they brought me food that was very good and a pitcher or water and a paper bag with fruit. After eating I lay on the small bed with my hands behind my head wondering if this safe feeling was temporary or just delaying the inevitable. I had made peace with death once; it would be an emotional setback to have to deal with those feeling again.

For now I felt safe. As I laid on the bed, I remembered one of the pastors at our church talking about the hand of God. He said you can always tell when the hand of God was on you. I wondered if this truly was the hand of God as I fell asleep for the first time since the meeting with the DEA. I got my first rest in days. The next morning, there was a knock on the door at the break of dawn. I heard the sound of keys as they unlocked the door. I was given breakfast and a change of underwear. There was not a word spoken between me and the man who delivered the food. I was still not allowed outside. I spent most of the day, looking out the small window facing the Potomac, trying to determine where I was. There was no visible structure in the distance. If you wanted to hide, this was the perfect place. There was one book in the cabin, the Bible. As I read the scriptures, tears rolled down my face. I thought about Raven. We agreed I would call her every day at noon at her mother's. I knew I would not be able to keep that commitment. Telling her that made her felt secure.

Hayes should have delivered the furniture by now. I hoped she found a place to put it. I thought of everything and anything, trying to take my mind off what was going to happen to me. It felt like the day had just begun when I could see the sun setting through my small window again. The next morning, I could hear one set of footsteps coming toward the door. A few minutes earlier, I had heard what sounded like two or three vehicles coming down the road at high speed. One knock on the door, and it was open. "Come with us," they said. I jumped up from the bed with my pants on and the undershirt they had given me, shoes and no socks. They took me toward the big house with one man in front and one behind. We entered a side door and went up two flights of stairs and into a large room beautifully decorated with fine furniture. They placed me outside of what looked like an office with the door open as one man went inside, and the other stayed with me. I could hear the conversation they were having through the door as if they wanted me to hear. As what sounded like a women's voice explaining her findings to what sounded like the man who questioned me when I was brought there.

"Sir, we have confirmed the information given by the civilian to be true, sir. Operation China White was launched by the CIA in early 1971; they had a problem with the methadone program. They were not having success getting treatment to the soldiers and civilians they thought needed it the most. People were not going to the methadone clinics. They concluded that too many restrictions were put in place by Congress in order to receive treatment. With crime increasing in major cities across the country at an alarming rate, the CIA thought the situation was getting out of hand and declared the crimes in major cities across the country a threat to national security. They used heroin to set up a network of dealers across the country within the last year. And as far as we can tell, they switched the product the dealers were getting from heroin to China White, which was code name for methadone."

"How in the hell did they switch heroin to methadone without anyone knowing what the hell was going on?" ("Oh my God," Katy said with her hand over her mouth.)

"With a small modification, it reacted just like heroin, sir. They knew at some point the switch would be discovered, hoping the methadone would react quickly to reduce crime and if each addict could receive five treatments the operation would be successful. It apparently worked. Crime has decreased in every major city in the country. We were able to obtained a sample. The room went silent for a moment. There is more, sir. This operation touches 1600. And once the operation was exposed, they shut it down, and the cleanup has begun. Most of the civilians involved have been eliminated. The CIA knows we have the civilian, sir. They were there when we extracted him. They are demanding his release. We contacted Sergeant Johnson in Hanoi. His request is we label him as family."

Things went silent for a few seconds before he said, "Well, this is a damned mess. Alright let's switch to let's make a deal. I want to get a message to Director Helm and tell him our position. Let him know we are holding family. Is that all major?"

"That all." I heard a door open and close, and then they brought me in the room.

"Son, you seem to have gotten yourself in one big mess. How old are you, son? I turned nineteen in March."

"Nineteen? How in the hell can you get in so much trouble at nineteen? Johnson is one of the best officers I have in the field. I trained him myself. He is the best! He is special, son. You understand. If it was anyone else, I would kick your drug-dealing ass to the wolves. You were playing a game way over your head, boy." That was the first time I had someone speak to me like a father expressing disgust. "Give him limited grounds access until we get this mess straightened out."

"That all?

"Hey," he said, "why are you not in the military, son?"

"I was turned down on a medical."

"We'll see about that. That's all." This time, they escorted me to my room, and they left the door open. Although the door was open, I wanted to lie on the bed and absorb what had just happened.

I thought about my brother-in-law Richard and the first time I saw him. I was twelve years old sitting on the backsteps of our home in Leland, Mississippi, one Saturday evening after cutting the grass when this man in uniform walked around the corner of our house. Our house was a shotgun house, and everyone entered through the back door because entering through the front door lets you in my mother's bedroom, and she didn't like that. I had never seen a black man in uniform in person before, only on TV. I was frozen as he walked closer, stopping within a feet away from me. He asked if my sister Selenia was home. His shoes were shined. His uniform was pressed without a wrinkle. I couldn't take my eyes off the shiny watch he had on his arm, and he could see I was fascinated by it. My mother walked out of the kitchen and looked him up and down, and then up and down again. Then asked him what he wanted with that intimidating voice she used when she wanted you to pay attention. I was surprised when the soldier was not afraid of her voice and walked up the steps toward her with his hand open to introduce himself to my mother. He talked to my mother for hours before Selenia got home. I could hear my mother laughing as he told her story after story. My sister was too young to date, but my mother let him stay and talk to her. Before he left, he gave me the watch off his arm. I remember it was a Seiko. He told me he got it in Japan. I had only read about Japan in the history books, and to think he had been there was amazing. The watch was the nicest thing I had ever owned. My sister would always talk about how smart Richard was. He spoke seven languages and taught self-defense to all the kids in their neighborhood growing up. I had no idea he was Special Forces. But when you looked at these men and Richard, it all fit. He was truly special. ("Thank God for Richard," Katy said.) I was there two more days before I was called back to the big house, and they took me straight to the man's office whose name I didn't know or anyone else's for that matter.

"Sit down, son," he said. "These men are going to take you back to where they found you." My heart dropped. I thought all this for nothing. Then he said, "You need to forget the last two years of your life. Totally remove them from your memory. Do you understand!"

"Yes, sir."

"You do not tell anyone!" He said, "You do not even mention the word *methadone* in a sentence. Do you understand me, son?"

"Yes, sir."

"These instructions I am giving you are the only things that will keep you alive. Then with his hand behind his back, he said, "Do you know what it is like owing the enemy a favor? That is what you cost me, son, and I don't like owing favors! Now when you get back to your car, you are going to find the three million dollars in the trunk gone. That money belongs to the United States government, son, not you! There is a war going on!" In the same breath, he said, "We left you the change. Now you need to leave Washington, DC, today and never look back! You need to thank Commander Johnson that you are still breathing. Take him away!"

One man put his arm under my arm and led me down the steps. They put me in the van and put the hood over my head and drove off taking me back to East Potomac Park. I could tell now it was an hour away wherever they had taken me. My car was parked nearly in the same place, and they threw me my keys, and one of them said good luck as he jumped in the van and drove away as fast as they had came in.

I sat on that bench and cried like a baby and thanked God for saving me. I made some promises to God on that bench that morning that I have kept to this day and one I would keep thirty two years later. I looked in the trunk and saw they had left the money Shannon had put on the kitchen counter. I thought about the $103,000 I had in the bank and decided not to claim it. I needed to follow the orders the man in the red hat had given me. I went to a pay phone to call Raven. I had not spoken to her since she left. I am sure she must think the worst by now. Her sister answered the phone. I didn't know which one. I just asked to speak to Raven. I could hear her call out to Raven, excited as loud footsteps rushed to the phone.

"Johnny, is that you? Yes, I am on my way to Winston Salem. I rented a house," she said, "and you are on the way?"

"Yes, I am leaving Washington as we speak. I will see you tonight. Did you take care of…?"

Before she could say another word, I said, "Yes, it's all over."

"The furniture came. I am getting the house ready for you. I can't wait to see you," she said with excitement in her voice. She gave me the phone number to the house she rented. I hung up and walked to my car when the phone I was just using rang. I froze with one foot in the car and the other on the ground. This was a pay phone. Why was it ringing? Remember this was, 1973 and there was no caller ID. There was no way Raven would be calling back. I didn't give her the number. I decided to answer it. The voice on the other end was my brother-in-law Richard. I knew his voice even though he never said who he was.

"Just listen," he said. "Over the next few years, you will be tested. They will send people up to you, and they will pretend to know you from the past and try to get you to speak about this time in your life. You can't be caught offguard and start talking about the past. You have to remember that this time in your life never existed." Every time I tried to speak to thank him, he would interrupt and continue talking. "The number you used, never use it again. It is not a get-out-of-jail-free card. Take care of yourself," he said, and the phone went dead. I knew I had just spoken to Richard, but I never got a chance to say hello or thank you.

Then I realized I had left the door to my car open. I got in and drove to Winston Salem, thanking and praising God for saving my life. I loved the house Raven had rented, and after hours of talking about our new life in Winston Salem, North Carolina, I had the best night's sleep I had in weeks. I woke up in a new city and a chance for a new life. Two weeks later, I called Fred. I had given him the money that was stored at my apartment and was hoping to retrieve it to finance our new life, only to learn from Fred he had a gambling problem. He loved to play a game called Georgia skin, and all my money was gone. I asked him if he sent Lewis's family his money and jewelry. He said he did. I had no way of checking, and if I did, I wouldn't have. I decided to go into business with my brother-in-law who owned the record store. I had given him money to improve his inventory on my last visit to Winston Salem. I convinced him the way he approached business would never work. Working at Mr. Men's, I was taught every phase of how to operate a business. We had a CPA on staff who taught me how to create a profit and loss statement, cash flow reports, balance sheets, and projections and how to indentify problems in business and fix them before they became bigger problems.

Over the next twenty-two years, I opened nine stores in Greensboro, Winston Salem, and Charlotte. In June of 1999, I was faced with taking the company through chapter 11; I had been through chapter 11 in 1981 and could do it again. This time, my heart wasn't in it. I was not happy with what the music industry had evolved into. Eighty percent of the music we sold in our stores was labeled with explicit lyric warnings. That was being bought by kids whose minds were young and impressionable. I felt selling this music contradicted everything I believed in. So I walked away in June 1999, not knowing what I was going to do or where my next paycheck would come from. With very little savings, I was sure I would be out of money within a year. But I decided to take my time to find out what I wanted to do with the rest of my life, and I wanted God to play a part in that decision. Raven and I had married and divorced in 1983. I gave her everything we had accumulated together in the divorce settlement. I wanted her to have a good life. I never told or discussed what happened in Washington, DC, with her. I wanted to keep her safe. I learned from that marriage that lust fades, but love endures to the end.

I married Phyllis, the love of my life, in 1996. Through her, I learned what true love really means. In my heart, I know she is the pure definition of the meaning of what a woman is. She rocks my world. Just looking at her makes me happy. And she was very supportive of my decision to close the stores, knowing the lifestyle we had created could not be supported on a flight attendants salary. But she never voiced any concern. I was sitting at home one afternoon after praying to God about what he wanted me to do with my life. I listened to a couple of tapes a friend had given me, by Kenneth Copeland. He talked about a man named Kenneth Hagen Sr. who was given a month to live, and God raised him from the bed of affliction and had given him life. Kenneth Hagen Sr. promised God if he healed him, he would preach the Word of God from one end of Texas to the other. It made me think about the promises I made to God twenty-four years earlier, sitting on that bench in East Potomac Park after He saved my life. I made the decision to get busy serving him for the rest of my life.

After laying quiet for a minute, Katy told me, "One day, you should write a book about this, and let history be the judge." My sister Katy died three months after hearing this story in 1986.

The End

At least I thought it was the end. I took a trip to New Orleans in April of 2000 to move my mother to new housing. It took a great deal of the money I had saved, but I knew it was something God wanted me to do. When I returned, my wife gave me a number to call, with no name. She told me the man said it was important that I call. I noticed the area code was for Atlanta. I dialed. The phone began to ring, and the voice that answered the phone sent chills throughout my whole body; it was Doc! He didn't have to say another word. I knew his voice, and after twenty-seven years, it was as if I had heard it yesterday.

"This is Johnny," I said. "Someone called my home and left this number for me to call.

"This is Doc."

"I know," I said.

"I was hoping you would come to Atlanta. There are some things I need to tell you before I die. The doctors have given me a few months to live, and for the last two weeks I have dreamed about you almost every night. I need to set the record straight. I told Doc there was no need. I had moved on, and those year were far removed from my life."

"I know," he said, "but not from mine. I promise the visit will be worth your while. Bring your wife, if you like. Think about it. Here is the address. I hope you decide to come." Phyllis could see I was visibly shaken after talking with Doc. This was the part of my life I never talked about with her or anyone else in my life other than my sister Katy. I told my wife it was an old friend I had not heard from in years; he was dying and asked if I would come and visit him.

"Well of course you will," she said.

"Let me pray about it," I said. "My steps are ordered by the Lord, and if it is his will, I'll make the trip."

"You mean we will make the trip," she said. That night I had a dream about Doc and had a peace beyond all understanding about going. I told my wife about the decision and called Doc to inform him I would be there on Saturday. It was only a four-hour drive, so I could make it a day trip. I didn't want to spend the night. We left early Saturday morning and arrived at Doc's house around one thirty in the afternoon. Before we could ring the doorbell, the door swung open, and there he was older and frail but with the same smile always painted on his face.

"Come in." This is my wife Sharon, my son Dayton, and daughter Linda."

"This is my wife Phyllis," I said.

"We were hoping you guys were hungry. Sharon suggested we go out and get some lunch. I suggested Chinese." Doc had a van, and we all climbed in, and the questions began from Phyllis and his family. I was not sure what Doc had told his family. But I knew I had not shared any parts of my life pertaining to Doc with Phyllis.

"Do you have any children?" Sharon asked.

"No," my wife said. "We have been married for four years, but we dated for years before we married. My husband is the only kid I have." The question never came up how Doc and I met. If it had, I was sure I would have let Doc tell the story. During lunch, I had flashbacks about my life in Washington, DC. It was a reflection as if it was a bad dream. We returned from lunch to Doc's house. It sits on a hill on six acres of land in Buckhead. Once at the top of the hill, there was a six-car garage. Off to the right were two tennis courts visible from the entrance. When we entered, you could tell from the hallway they spared no expense decorating their home. We entered a sunken great room that was separated by a one-hundred-foot hallway and a five-thousand-gallon salt water tank with beautiful fish. Some I had never seen before. Sharon offered to show my wife the rest of the house, and Doc and I made our way to a side room that overlooked a large swimming pool.

"What have you been doing?" Doc asked.

"After moving to Winston Salem, I went into the music business and opened a chain of music stores I operated for twenty-two years. I closed them in 1999, and since then, I have been doing some consulting work. But my real job is working for God and Son, telling everyone that wants to listen about Jesus!"

"You're a preacher?" Doc asked.

"No, I am a minister."

"What's the difference?" he asked.

"A preacher has a congregation he is responsible for. A minister for God is responsible for telling the world about Jesus every chance he gets and anyway they can."

"I am an atheist," Doc said. "That explained a lot. I had prayed how I would witness to him, but God never gave me an answer. Now I knew I was not supposed to. All I have seen in the world, how can there be a God?" he said.

I smiled and said, "With all I have seen in the world, how can there not be?" Then this expression came across Doc's face when he wanted you to listen, and his eyes turned to stone.

"I had no choice," he said. "The CIA had me dead to rights. I could cooperate and keep my life and family intact or not and lose everything. I chose to cooperate. They gave me this speech about God and the country, for the greater good, and sacrificing the few for the many to live. I had faith in the methadone treatment of the addict. I owned five medical treatment centers. The addict was not coming in for treatment, too much red tape. Those people don't carry ID or anything else. They are just looking for the next high. I am not proud of what I had to do, but given the choice, I would do it all over again. I often wondered what happened to you?" he said. "Later, I learned you were connected and was able to get out. I was glad to hear that. I will never say I am sorry for what we did; we saved a lot of lives. Yes, a few lives were lost, but that's how America was built." Listening to Doc talk, I knew he was sorry, and that's the reason he needed to see me, to confess. Not believing in God, there was no other way to release his pain. Now I know why God wanted me to come. I thought I was over this time in my life, that I had moved on. God knew this chapter was not over, and I had to face this demon to make me stronger. There were many questions I would have loved to ask Doc. Did you choose me, or did I choose you? Did the CIA know Lewis's and Cheyenne's operation before I met with them? Of course they did.

After he stopped talking, I said, "Doc, I have no idea what you are talking about."

He smiled and said, "Of course you don't," knowing that was the only answer I could give him. "I told you I would make this trip worth your while. I don't know how you are set for cash, but there is one million in that case." Doc was pointing to a small piece of luggage. "Take it if you need it. I surely needed it, but one thing is for sure, I was not jumping back across that spiritual line that God had delivered me from."

I told him, "I'm okay. Thanks." I saw my wife and Sharon walking the grounds. We joined them as they made their way inside. There were walls of artist's painting throughout the house. But Doc took us into this room decorated with African art. In the corner was a mummy he paid thirty thousand dollars for that was supposed to have healing powers. On one wall were masks, some dating back three thousand years, he said. My wife was drawn to this one in particular. Doc told her that one was two thousand years old. We finished the tour, and it was getting late.

We had some refreshments, and it was time to leave. Doc and Sharon walked us to the door and said their good-bye. They gave my wife a gift and asked that she not open it until we got home.

On our way home, Phyllis talked about what a nice woman Sharon was. "She's a doctor you know? How many other wealthy friends do you have that I haven't met?"

"I can think of a few," I said. When we arrived home, the first thing my wife did was open her gift. It was the two-thousand-year-old African mask she had admired from Doc's collection.

Doc passed away one year after our visit. I did not attend his funeral.